GLASS

TWENTIETH-CENTURY DESIGN

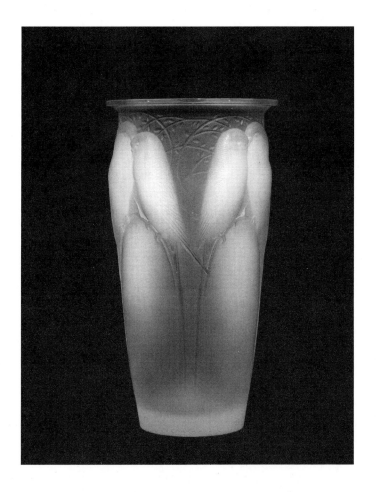

Fredrick Cooke

E.P. DUTTON New York

To my mother and in memory
of my father.

First published, 1986, in the United States
by E.P. Dutton

Published in the United States by E.P.
Dutton, a division of New American
Library, 2 Park Avenue, New York, N.Y.
10016.

Library of Congress Catalog Card Number:
86-71624

ISBN: 0-525-24464-6 (Cloth)
ISBN: 0-525-48261-X (DP)

OBE

10 9 8 7 6 5 4 3 2 1
First Edition

Designed by Richard Crawford
Typeset by TJB Photosetting Limited,
South Witham, Lincolnshire, England
Printed in Great Britain.

Other books in the series:
FURNITURE
CERAMICS
FABRICS AND WALLPAPERS

Forthcoming titles:
ELECTRICAL APPLIANCES
OFFICE FURNITURE

*Overleaf: 'Ceylan' – a pressed glass vase with relief of birds made in opal glass,
designed by Réné Lalique, c.1925.*

CONTENTS

INTRODUCTION

DURING the past 200 years the art of glass-making has undergone considerable change, Yet paradoxically many of the working methods employed by today's glass-makers have remained fundamentally the same for over 2,000 years. Most of today's techniques and tools used in the manufacture of studio production-glass would be very familiar to craftsmen of an earlier age. By contrast, in the large industrial plants, where great numbers of vessels are produced on computer operated machines to satisfy the needs of a vast world market, the technology would be beyond their comprehension.

Division of labour was a feature of glass manufacture long before Josiah Wedgwood pioneered its introduction at his Etruria pottery in the

Cut glass vases from the 'Frensham' range designed by David Hammond for Thomas Webb & Sons, 1970s.

late 18th century. The usual argument that such specialization resulted in workers being divorced from both the means and the reason of their labour did not hold true in glass manufacture. Each craftsman had a clear idea of the various stages of production and the importance of his role in relation to the whole making process.

Before the middle of the last century, the design of a glass vessel was an integral part of the traditional working practice of a chair. Though design was the responsibility of the gaffer, it was evolved in the glasshouse as a consequence of the needs of the market on the one hand and familiarity with materials and working methods on the other.

This shared creative act — design-by-making — was experimental rather than inventive. The design of artefacts was realised by a process of trial and error in which working methods and fortuitous accidents, rather than the application of a logi-

cal creative system, dictated form and visual character. This same method of creativity through discovery was used to great advantage by Maurice Marinot in his Hot-glass work of the 1930s and is favoured by many studio glass artists today. Marinot liked to discover and develop qualities whilst working with the glass in its molten form. He spoke of 'freezing' the creative act at the point when he was satisfied with the statement taking shape before him at the furnace mouth.

Today, glass-making falls into two main categories. One is mass-produced glass made by machines in which standardization of form and quality are considered essential; and the other is studio production glass. Here the artist seeks to develop the intrinsic qualities of glass in a unique manner.

The history of glass-making is rich in such variations in practice and belief. As with all aspects of design history, the pattern of change is not a simple linear development from one period of creative activity to another, but a complex interaction of new and old values. One can discern an evolutionary process in the history of design and its effect is evident in the development of glass-making. The cultural schism between craft production and industrial production is one obvious facet. This, unintentionally, led to the emergence of design as a creative activity in its own right, transcending the boundaries of craft practice. It is a phenomenon of great importance to our understanding of the place of glass-making in a modern, industrial society.

The glass products with which most people are familiar are those of the container and domestic glass industries. Few consumers know anything of the circumstances in which the products, so essential to their domestic environment, were designed and produced. Their critical judgments are made on the basis of functional adequacy, external appearance and comparative value for money. These issues are important in making consumer choices, but they do little to provide a useful critical framework within which to evaluate the products of industrialized society.

In order, then, to evaluate the state of the historical evolution of design in glass of a given period, it is necessary to consider the products in relation to the wider social and cultural circumstances which prevailed at the time.

In the past 30 years the literature on glass-making has been extended considerably in all fields. Many admirable works have been written both for the serious collector and the student of glass history. Some writers have sought to address themselves to the methodological problems outlined above, but none have had the design history of glass of the modern industrial era as their main object. The material dealt with in this book is intended to give a balanced overview of the relationship between design and glass manufacture in the industrial age.

THE NATURE OF GLASS

GLASS is found in many forms in our man-made environment, and is one of the commonest synthetic materials in everyday domestic life. Its presence in the form of tablewares, windows, containers, ornaments and, more recently, as a material used to insulate our homes is taken for granted. Although the number and variety of products made from glass has significantly increased during the 20th century the material has played a key part in the manufacture and design of domestic articles since earliest times.

Throughout most of the history of glass-making the process of design was fully integrated into the manufacturing process. Before the industrialization of society in the 19th century the form of a glass was achieved by the traditional procedure of 'design-by-making'. Creativity and practice were organically related parts of a craft tradition. Variety of form and decoration were achieved by modifying the ways in which the glass was manipulated at given stages in the making process. By the end of the 19th century this practice had changed and the creative act of design was carried out by draughtsmen. In many instances designs were produced by men with little or no practical experience of glass-making.

The traditional practices of the glasshouse were passed on through a long period of apprenticeship. Training often started at about nine years of age and, as with other crafts, apprentices commonly came from families associated with glass-making over many generations.

The adoption of wholly different forms normally occurred as a result of contact with glass-makers from other regions with different traditions of practice. Innovation was not merely a matter of glassmakers copying foreign forms but rather of adapting such forms to their traditional practice. Sometimes change was more radical, as when one tradition supplanted another. However most change was gradual and took place during transitional periods often lasting generations. Although regional variations were strong the fundamental nature of most glass was common to them all. Generations of glassmakers belonging to different traditions employed very similar methods and techniques in fashioning glass.

The nature of the material and the processes of manufacture were essential determinants of design.

Almost all glass objects have been produced from a synthetic glass formed by melting raw materials. Glass does exist in a ready-made or natural state. But natural glass is only found in very small quantities. The most common type is Obsidian, formed when molten lava is quenched and solidified by water to form a dense black glass. It is found wherever volcanic activity has occurred. Like flint-stones, glass was used by Stone-age man to make basic tools such as scrapers and arrow heads. Much rarer occurrences of natural glass are the remains of meteorites and glassy masses formed by lightening striking desert sands. Interesting though these substances are it is with glass manufactured from a mixture of raw materials that man has created both some of the most prized, and most commonplace artefacts of his cultural development.

It is the intrinsic qualities of glass which have enabled it to adapt fully to the changing needs of man. There are many types of metal, the glass-makers' term for the molten glass. Some were developed over generations of craft practice in regions where different raw materials were available. Others were developed to satisfy particular design criteria, as in the case of the heat-resisting borosilicate glass used in the production of Pyrex. The different characteristics of these metals affect the form, colour and surface qualities of the final product. They are critical to both manufacture and design.

Although glass appears to be solid and have a permanent shape it is, in fact, a liquid which is subject to constant change. Scientists refer to glass as a 'super-cooled' liquid which, irrespective of the size of the piece of glass, is composed of a single molecule. Because glass has only two surfaces to interrupt the passage of light it is super-transparent.

Glass is an excellent reflector of light though it is not generally realized that the surfaces of glass reflect light back into the body of the glass as well as outwards. Light passing through a sheet of glass is refracted onto a different course. These qualities of refraction and reflection have been exploited by scientists and glass-cutters alike. Long before scientists like Sir Isaac Newton were able to explain the principles of reflection and refraction they had been used in producing cut-glass, trick mirrors, and lenses.

When heated to about 1140°C glass becomes a soft toffee like mass that can be scooped up on an iron rod and bent, stretched, squeezed, blown and pressed or moulded into shape. It is the ductility of the heated metal that has been the single most important reason for the continuing success of glass as a production material throughout its 6,000-year history.

The constituents of any recipe for glass have remained fundamentally unchanged from those used before man applied scientific methods to gain knowledge of their chemical and physical properties. The main ingredient is silica, which on its own melts at about 1700°C. An alkaline flux, like soda or potash, is added to lower the melting point to about 1450°C, and lime is added for hardness. Cullet (off-cuts and broken pieces of used glass) often forms part of the recipe. The addition of cullet is said to improve a new batch of metal and it reduces the time taken to fuse raw materials since it also acts as a flux to the silica. The working temperature is generally about 1180°C for blown glass and approximately 1250°C for pressed or cast glass.

Prior to the 17th century two basic types of metal existed. In one the metal was fused using a soda flux and in the other a potash flux was used. Historians of glass have come to know these two traditions of manufacture as the 'soda' glass tradition on the one hand, and the 'potash' or 'forest' glass tradition on the other.

The 'soda' tradition probably originated in Mesopotamia and spread throughout the Middle East as a result of conquest and trade. Soda glass was highly valued for its clarity and brightness, and for a standard of craftmanship the West struggled for many years to equal. By the end of the 13th century the fame of 'Damascus' glass, as all Islamic glass was called, was known across Europe. Glass of a similar metal, also decorated with enamels, was made in the West by the middle of the 14th century but it was very inferior to real Damascus glass.

It was the 'potash' tradition, with its very plastic hot-glass forms and coarse metal, that dominated glass manufacture throughout the Mediaeval period in central and northern Europe. This glass, also called 'Forest' glass, is normally strong green in colour and coarse in texture, being full of bubbles and seeds (flecks of hard glass). Forest glass vessels are generally of a cruder form than those made from soda glass.

Although there have been some modifications, due to technological and scientific development, the principal methods of forming glass have continued essentially unchanged. Such methods are free-blowing or off-hand work, mould-blowing and pressing.

It is the process of free-blowing that most people associate with the making of glass. It is still used to make the finest domestic glass but has long been replaced by mechanical production for most domestic wares and containers. However, since the 1960s there has been considerable expansion in the manufacture of studio-production glass which relies upon hand-crafting methods of forming and decorating.

The design of studio-production glass is more often than not achieved by developing ideas in exploratory drawings. During this conceptual process the craftsman draws on his experience of manipulating glass to assist in the development of the design idea. The idea is then explored by producing proto-types, modifying the idea until a final statement is achieved. This is the mode of design and glass-making practice which is taught in the glass-making studios of colleges and polytechnics.

The decoration of glass involving the use of colours and special effects is achieved in the same way; exploring the possibilities of techniques of which the glassmaker has experience. The dependence upon 'fortuitous blemishes' is an important and dynamic aesthetic of this mode of design activity. The element of chance makes production-studio glass, of even the most repetitive kind, a unique experience of unending pleasure. The slight variations and inaccuracies of free-blown glass are an essential aspect of its broad appeal.

The primary tool of the studio glass-maker is the blowing iron — a hollow steel tube. It is only one of a set of about a dozen tools that are used by a chair (team) of glass-makers.

Central to all glass-blowing is the gaffer's chair. This is the work bench at which most of the forming takes place. In a large studio its occupant is served by a team of makers, each highly skilled in his particular role in the production of a design. The gaffer is responsible for managing these separate elements of the making process. The chair varies in size. In a small studio it may consist of only two craftsmen taking it in turns to sit at the chair. In larger studios a team consists of four to seven men.

The sequence of related tasks by which a glass is made varies according to its design and the number of component parts. It is quite common for the components of more than one piece of glass to be in production at the same time. Before one form is finished and put into the lehr (kiln) to toughen, the bowl of another is started off by a servitor. The manufacture of blown glass is as interactive as a piece of drama or a dance. Success is dependent on the skills of the whole group and on effective timing.

A drinking glass with a 'knopped' stem may have as many as five component parts. Each component has to be prepared to the exact requirements of the gaffer at exactly the right time. Timing is important because the metal remains workable only for a short period and although glass can be 'warmed-in' again, it takes up valuable making time.

Moulds are used in making many types of products, from the unique productions of the studio artist to the common milk bottle. They can be used in a single process to blow the final form or they can be introduced as part of a more complex process merely to give a surface pattern to a gather of glass which is then free-blown to its final form.

It is in the manufacture of production-glass that the studio glass-maker most often uses moulds. They enable the accurate reproduction of forms but also offer considerable savings in time. The use of moulds is very important to the manufacture of sets of objects where consistency of size is an essential concern of the blower.

Studio glass-makers also use mould-blowing to produce unique pieces. In these cases the moulds are either used once only or can be altered by changing elements from which they are composed. They are also used to obtain a basic form which is then rendered unique by further manipulation and hot-work additions of glass.

Although very different in some aspects from the automated industrial process the studio method of producing mould blown production glass in a single blow is based upon the same fundamental principles.

In industrial mass-production, cast-iron rather than wooden moulds are used in machines which use compressed air to blow the forms. The moulds are so designed as to enable the cracking-off and trimming of the form in one fast and continuous process.

The automated process requires a continuous flow of metal. The raw ingredients of the glass are fused in a specially designed furnace and the resultant metal flows into a large enclosed tank. As it progresses to the outflow-end it cools to a working temperature. The glass is fed to a turret machine in shots sufficient to make a form and leave little or no waste. Modern manufacture of pressed-glass also makes use of moulds continuously supplied with metal in a full automated production cycle. Two types of mould are used. Flat wares like Pyrex dishes are made in block moulds which consist of three parts – mould, ring and plunger. The mould splits horizontally around the rim of the form. Hollow wares such as jugs are made in split moulds – two or more parts hinged together, a ring and a plunger. This sort is used for asymmetrical and undercut forms such as those with handles and knobs. The mould splits both around the rim and vertically, i.e. along the length of the handle. Although such processes are very efficient in production they are also very limiting on design and represent a high level of capital expenditure. The moulds alone can account for more than 30 per cent of the cost of production.

The decorative processes of glass manufacture fall into two main groups – hot work and cold work. Except for enamelling, hot work decoration is always undertaken as part of the making process whether by hand or machine. Cold work decoration can be done at any time and far away from the site of manufacture.

Hot work decoration is most often connected with colour. Colour and opacity in glass are achieved by adding small proportions of metallic oxides to the batch after the initial melt has been achieved. Metal coloured in this way is called pot-metal because the colour is formed in the glass whilst it is still in its melting pot. Coloured glassware can be made from pot-metal but it is very costly and the cheaper method of colouring glass, using a thin layer of pot-metal colour over the glass, is more common.

Coloured glass was made long before glass-makers discovered the technique of producing a pure clear glass. Even without the addition of colouring oxides, glass had a 'natural' colour. The raw materials from which the metal was made contained many impurities, including traces of iron oxide. Quite small amounts of iron will give glass a green tinge.

Antimony or manganese dioxide can be added to the batch of metal to clarify it. These oxides counteract the effects of the ferrous iron impurities by inducing oxidization at about 1140°C. In actual fact the resulting glass isn't wholly without colour and continual exposure to direct sunlight over a very long period of time has caused much early clear glass to turn a very pale rose or straw colour, a process known as solarization.

Greens and yellows resulting from the presence of iron impurities were among the earliest colours known to glass-makers. The degree to which early glass-makers could control such colour is not known. The colour develops in proportion to temperature and the length of time high temperatures are maintained. In addition the glass-makers discovered that they could control colour by increasing or diminishing the amount of oxygen in the furnace. This would produce yellower or bluer greens respectively.

Iron oxide was also added separately as a colouring agent to produce very dark, virtually black glass. The

dark green of wine bottles is caused by a high concentration of iron oxide in the metal.

Blue also appears in glass from the earliest times. Indeed many archaeologists are of the opinion that since glass-making seems to have developed in close proximity to the working of copper, blue was probably the first known colour. Both copper and cobalt oxide were used to produce a range of blue glasses in the countries bordering the eastern mediterranean about 2000 B.C. The degree to which either or both were present depended upon the type of blue sought by the craftsman. As with the production of green glass the glass-maker could change the colour by varying the furnace atmosphere. In this case it produced a range from a colder and more intense blue to a turquoise blue.

One of the most remarkable, and

Engraving of the interior of a 19th-century glass house showing the various activities of the teams working for the masters seated at their 'chairs'.

certainly costly methods of colouring glass was the production of red or ruby colour using a colloidal gold. The most famous example of this sort of glass is the 4th-century Lycurgus cup. The cup has a dull khaki colour when viewed under direct light but when light is transmitted through it, the suspended gold particles give it a rich ruby colour. More commonly, cupreous oxide was used in a similar manner. Both techniques were re-discovered at the end of the 17th century by the German glass-maker Johann Kunckel whose name is still associated with the best quality pot-metal glass today.

These basic colouring oxides are still the most commonly used in present day manufacture although a number of new ones have been added in the past 100 years and the range of colours available to glass-makers is greater than at any time of its history. Other hot decorative methods include rolling particles of glass into the surface and then covering them with another layer of glass in a process called 'casing'. Colour can also be applied by melting pot-metal from a rod to form patches on the surface. Layers of coloured metal can be encased over the whole surface and exposed by cutting the surfaces back by acid etching or by cutting and engraving.

The decorative techniques most commonly used on glass in its cold state are cutting, engraving, acid etching, sand blasting and hot and cold enamelling.

Cut glass is made from a highly refractive lead crystal metal. Forms are made with sufficient thickness to provide a substantial body for the cutter to work from. An experienced cutter can achieve great variety in decoration employing only a narrow range of cuts.

Most cut pattern is achieved in stages employing grinding stones and wood or cork polishing wheels. The main elements and divisions of the design are marked down and cut using roughing stone. The cuts are made by holding the glass vessel against an abrasive wheel which is kept wet so as to lubricate the grind and keep both wheel and vessel from overheating. There are three main shapes of stone, the 'hollow cut' which has a round edge, the 'bevel cut' with a V-shaped edge, and the 'panel cut' which has a flat edge. The glass cutter works above the cutting wheel which is turning away from him in a clockwise direction. The cutting stones produce matt facets and cuts called 'gray-cuts'. These are polished to a brilliant finish using finer stones and cork or wooden polishing wheels coated with polishing pastes.

Unlike the cutter, the glass engraver works below the wheel, looking at the front side of his design. The wheels, which are of copper, are graded in diameter and, like the cutter's stones, they have edges of varying shape. Unlike the cutter's stones these copper wheels are not in themselves abrasive. A slurry made from an abrasive powder, usually silicon carbide, mixed with oil is dribbled onto the spinning wheel.

The most common form of engraving consists of making matt patterns on the surface of glass. Much less common today is a technique called intaglio or 'tag'. Intaglio engraving cuts deep into the surface of the glass. The decoration has the appearance of a miniature sculptural relief which, although it is carved into the thickness of the glass, seems to stand out from it.

Patterns are also engraved by scratching and tapping on the surface of glass using either diamond or tungsten carbide tips. The technique has become increasingly popular in recent years, especially for commemorative glasses. It is often used in combination with simple wheel engraving using a flexible hand-held drive.

Acid etching is done by applying a protective coating of resist through which the desired pattern is cut and then exposed to the caustic effects of hydrofluoric acid

By varying the type of material used for the resist and the strength of the acid a variety of textures can be achieved. A cocktail of hydrofluoric and sulphuric acid mixed with water can be used to give glass a very brightly polished surface whereas concentrated hydroflouric acid will cut very coarse textures deep into the body of the thickest glass.

Sand blasting is often used instead of acid etching in both factory and studio. It is very much safer and more convenient to use. As with acid etching the design is cut into the exposed surface of the glass. A stream of compressed air is used to blast sand or some other abrasive grit at the surface gradually cutting it back. The quality and the degree of the 'etch' is controlled by varying the sharpness of the grit and the length of exposure and force of the blast.

The application of colour to the surface glass has most commonly been achieved by painting enamels on the surface. This painting can be done using either cold or hot enamels. Cold enamelling makes use of resin bonded paints. Early examples are not very resistent to the effects of moisture or heat and the technique tended to be restricted to ornamental glass until very recently. The development of new epoxy resin bonded paints for metal protection has provided glass manufacturers with paints that are cheaper to make and apply to glass. In the past five years glasses decorated using these new super-resistant paints have increased their share of the market. The designs are often screen printed directly onto the surface of the glass or applied as slide-on transfers which are baked onto the surface at a much lower temperature than is needed to fuse hot enamels. Hot enamels are also applied by screening and as transfers but unlike paints they are then fused into the surface of the glass. Compared with the earlier cold enamels, hot enamels are very resistant to the effects of detergents and abrasion but do not always out-perform the new epoxy paints.

It is in the application of their ingenuity and skill that the designer and craftsman have harnessed the fundamental nature of the metal to express the unique values of their age.

Design has become a focus for market identity in recent years to the extent that some objects seem only to exist to fill a vacuum created by the silky veneer of advertising copy. The term 'design' has taken on a new meaning. It is now a value rather than a creative process – a label to be hung on products which have a high status rarely associated with ethics like truth to material or the democratization of beauty which have underpinned design activity since the Bauhaus.

The effect of 'above the line' activity can be seen in the way in which glassware is marketed by manufacturers active at all levels. It is so vigorous that one's visual concept of a product often coincides more with the photograph in the brochure than the real object.

The advertising material surrounding design is more transient than the products it promotes and very little survives even from the 60s. The glass itself, being more durable, has outlasted the claims that were made for it and can now be seen more objectively within its historical context.

2

THE FORMATIVE YEARS:

ART VERSUS INDUSTRY

THE Industrial Revolution, which had already made its irreversible mark on English society in the 18th century, came much later to glass manufacture than to other industries. It was the 19th century which was to be the great age of change in glassmaking. New scientific knowledge enabled changes to be made in the refining and synthesis of raw materials which affected the volume and range of metals that were used. Mechanization on a large scale was introduced in the 1880s which was the first time that the manufacturing conditions under which glass was made had changed substantially in over 200 years.

In addition, the century witnessed other changes of much greater importance to glass manufacture and design. The growth of the middle classes and the increasing spending power of the lower market drew many different responses from manufacturers. The shift from an agrarian economy to one based on manufacturing affected the whole pattern of retailing. Many new firms relied on varied forms of financing unknown in previous times, and the relationship between the applied arts and the commercial fabric of the economy was more deep rooted and far reaching than ever before. In England, many mid-century glasshouses were capitalized on the security of family landholdings, in some instances using credit raised against smallholdings and animal stock. In America the clearance of land and the exploitation of natural resources, like timber and coal, brought immense industries into being in the developing mid-western cities, such as Pittsburgh and Toledo. Many of these larger concerns were joint stock companies and some were financed by public lotteries.

By the 1830s Industrialization had become an essential element of international trade and development. Commercial competition between countries led to the staging of international exhibitions on a scale never before contemplated. The political importance of such events, with their focus on nationalism, was quickly established. The desire to produce and display goods that combined the very latest technological developments with the highest level of design became something of a patriotic duty.

Whilst these 'state of the art' exhibitions were intended to attract attention to nations as a whole, they were also of considerable commercial importance to individual manufacturers. They provided an opportunity for ostentatious display of their abilities in ways not afforded by the usual scale of manufacture.

As the century progressed, the degree to which mechanization affected the social structure of the work place increased. Concern about the relationship between manufacture and design, initially expressed by a few people in England, found an increasing amount of support in other countries. The debate on 'art versus industry' developed into a moral and aesthetic movement which was ultimately to have far reaching implications for the development of industrial design in its many varied forms.

During the early 19th century the English glass trade had suffered under the imposition of a heavy tax on flint glass. The tax proved a hindrance to the development of glass manufacture in Britain during one of the most important periods of industrial growth. The tax was finally repealed in 1847, largely due to the efforts of Apsley Pellat whose family firm had a worldwide reputation for high quality cut glass.

The period of expansion that followed the ending of the tax encouraged British manufacturers to import foreign expertise in technology and craftsmanship. In particular they brought in experts from Europe, where glass manufacturers had been free to experiment with a wide range of metals, especially coloured pot metals. Robert Chance, the owner of large glasshouses at Nailsea near Bristol, and at Smethwick near Birmingham, brought in a French expert on coloured glass called Georges Bontemps. He and his men were to enable the production of stained glass of a quality not seen in England since the middle ages.

Although English cut glass had dominated the market for flint glass tablewares throughout the world, English coloured glass (with the sole exception of the blue and green crystal made and cut in Bristol) was of little consequence. On the continent, German and Bohemian glass in the bourgeois-romantic style called 'Biedermeier' was the dominant fashion at least until the 1850s. It was characterized by coloured enamel painting and engraved designs of a pretty and 'folksy' kind. In the studios of Samuel Mohn, in Dresden and Vienna, painters of great skill were used to decorate glasses in his style which were signed by him. The style was very detailed and decorative. He also made use of engraved transfer prints which were then hand painted.

The Bohemian glassworks of Novy Hrady and Novy Svet, belonging to Count George Buoquoy, were distinguished for their production of a red and black Hyalith metal imitating Wedgwood's 'roso antico' and 'Egyptian black'. Friederich Egermann used both metals to produce marbled patterned glass he called Lithyalin. The development did not remain a secret for long and by 1850 glass of the same type, resembling agates and other semi-precious stones, was being manufactured in many parts of Europe.

Egermann's major commercial breakthrough was with the use of stains in the 1820s. The thin coating of pot-metal of either ruby, amethyst, or yellow, proved very popular with intaglio engravers and cutters. Egermann employed over 200 craftsmen in the 1840s and his coloured glass was sold worldwide. Like other Bohemian glass manufacturers he started to produce pastel 'alabaster' and 'opal' metals of the sort made fashionable by French houses in the late 1830s.

Important though these experiments and developments were to the future of European glass it was the art of engraving that was to prove Bohemia's most valued and influential export. After a period of decline at the end of the century engraving came to dominate the Bohemian home market until the 1840s.

August Bohm worked at Meistersdorf before leaving to work firstly in Stourbridge, Hamburg and finally America. He, like other engravers, was to export Bohemian techniques in their search for larger and more lucrative outlets for their skills. The engravers Franz Eisert and Frederick Kny were to play very important roles in the development of not only intaglio engraving but also cameo carving in England.

At the beginning of the 19th century the American glass industry, despite an already large market for consumer products consisted of only nine glasshouses. By 1820 the number had risen to forty, most of them opening after the successful war with the British confirmed American independence. By the 1840s this number had more than trebled in its attempts to satisfy a rapidly expanding market now spreading out across the continent. The most essential task facing the American industry was that of satisfying market needs that for too long had been held to ransome by foreign, mostly English, manufacturers. The major contribution this as yet infant industry made was the development of cheap mechanical means of production unfettered by a dearth of skilled labour.

The first references to pressed glass appear in newspaper advertisements of 1819 and the earliest known patent was taken out for the production of furniture knobs by John Bakewell of the Pittsburgh Flint Glass Manufactory. Bakewell and Co. was one of the three major American pressed glassmakers, the others being the South Boston Crown Glass Co. and the New England Glass Co. By 1830 the other two companies and a number of smaller manufacturers had taken out similar patents.

Pressed glass exhibited at the New York City Industrial Fair of 1829 was written about by an English visitor, James Boardman, who was collecting information for his thesis on 'America and the Americans'. *"The most novel article was the pressed glass which was far superior, both in design and execution, to anything of the kind I have ever seen in London or elsewhere. The merit of its invention is due to the Americans and it is likely to prove one of great national importance."*

Early moulds for pressed glass were hand carved from wood. These were quickly replaced by moulds cast from brass or iron. The iron moulds, first patented by Joseph Magoun in 1847, produced a rather coarse surface in the finished glass.

When pressing was first introduced to produce cheap domestic glass the designs were taken from English and European lead crystal cut-glass. Early examples, mostly flat wares, were made in clear lead crystal. The metal tended to wrinkle on the surface of the moulds and, partly to disguise such flaws, a new style of design was introduced by the mouldmakers. The 'Lacy' style of glass was made by a number of companies but is especially associated with the Boston & Sandwich Glass Co. Lacy or Sandwich glass is very decorative comprising of very detailed ornament and backgrounds covered in fields of beads creating a stippled effect that masked any faults. Very soon the introduction of mechanical presses and improved iron moulds resulted in a proliferation of new designs.

Pressed glass was already being manufactured in England by the 1830s. Apsley Pellat applied for a patent in 1831 and Richardson's of Stourbridge were making patented pressed wares in 1834. Both companies exhibited at the Great Exhibition of 1851 in competition with New England Glass Company and the Boston & Sandwich Glass Company. At the New York World Exhibition three years later pressed glass dominated the American manufacturers section. Souvenirs made from pressed glass were produced for all major exhibitions. The Philadelphia Centenary Exhibition was commemorated with copies of the Liberty Bell. In England similar patriotic issues of Landseers Lions and a model of Britannia were issued for all Exhibitions and State Jubilees.

Hand pressing was already used in 18th-century Europe to make small solid items like knobs and buttons. Larger items using moulds were made at the French factory of Baccaratt by 1825 and by 1829 in Belgium by the firm of Val St. Lambert. In Bohemia the firm of Johann Meyr was the first to make pressed glass but later the process was taken up by other glassworks.

By 1864 steam powered pressing was introduced in America. Its introduction was to force even more changes in working methods. Steam power had been used in cutting shops in England and Europe since the beginning of the century. Rows of cutting lathes could be run from one machine, and were responsible for the somewhat monotonous use of crosshatched all-over mitre cutting, that required a low level of skill to produce.

As the century progressed manufactured goods played an increasingly important part in the expansion of national economies. Competition between manufacturing countries increased as a matter of national pride spurred on by the growth of large scale exhibitions of manufactured goods.

The applied arts received a major boost in 1848 when Prince Albert was elected President of the Royal Society of Arts and the initiative for a major national exhibition gathered momentum. The first major exhibition of industrial products, the Birmingham Exhibition of 1849, focused national interest on the products of glass-makers in Stourbridge and Birmingham. The Birmingham glass industry had grown to considerable size in thirty years especially in the production of coloured glass and pressed glass. Pressed glass by Rice Harris & Sons, George Bacchus & Sons, and Lloyd & Summerfield were illustrated in the *Art Journal* and the *Journal of Design and Manufactures.* Journals and papers played an increasingly important part in the promotion and marketing of manufacturers. Together with reports and catalogues to the exhibitions they also provided an opportunity for criticism. The glass exhibition in Birmingham and later at the Great Exhibition attracted much criticism from aesthetic and social reformers.

During the 1840s there had been a revival of interest in Gothic art and design. This nostalgic revival of patriotic forms drew much criticism from the architect A. W. N. Pugin, among others and it was in this critical climate that the Royal Society of Arts held its Exhibition of Ancient and Mediaeval Art in 1850. It included examples of Venetian glass from the Felix Slade Collection as well as examples of Islamic glass from the 14th century. The exhibition was intended to provide manufacturers and the public with an opportunity to study ancient styles, and to educate public taste.

The Exhibition of the Industry of All the Nations of 1851 — The Great Exhibition — was the first to include manufactured goods from all over the world. Almost all the leading glass makers in Europe and England exhibited as well as a number of American companies. The Crystal Palace, in which the exhibition was housed, was itself an important example of the state of English architectural engineering. The iron and glass building represented the 'state of the art' in cooperation between Art and Industry. It was certainly the single largest feat of manufacture. The glass panes, measuring over a million square feet were produced in about six months by an army of glass blowers at the Chance Bros factories in Smethwick near Birmingham.

This was the first time that so many products of different industries

Below: Fountain in cut lead crystal by F. & C. Osler. Exhibited in the Fountain Court of the Great Exhibition in 1851.

could be compared and evaluated by so wide a public. Some items were made specially for the exhibition but the majority of exhibits were items taken out of normal production. The Birmingham company of F. & C. Osler constructed an enormous cut-glass fountain over 20 feet high which formed the centrepiece of the exhibition. The exhibition was of extraordinary importance as a focus of public taste. Over six million people visited the site in the space of five months and the *Art Journal* catalogue, crammed with illustrations, spread that knowledge to an even wider public.

The most common exhibits in the glass court, coloured and cut glass wares, were present in equal amounts. Manufacturers seized on the opportunity to display the full range of their latest developments. The Bohemian exhibitors displayed a great variety of coloured, cut, and intaglio engraved glass; as did the only French exhibitor, Clichy.

Following the repeal of the glass tax, rapid developments in the formulation and manufacture of new metals had taken place in England. The Birmingham glasshouses of George Bacchus & Sons, and Rice Harris &

Right: Page from the Art Journal catalogue to the Great Exhibition of 1851, illustrating glass exhibited by English manufacturers.

Son, together with David Greathead & Green of Stourbridge and Apsley Pellat of London all displayed a wide range of colours reflecting the influence of Bohemian and French manufacturing practice. In the glass section of the exhibition guide the following comment was made about the effect

that the excise had had on experimental work in glass and the positive steps taken by manufacturers after its repeal:

"..no exemption being permitted even for the purpose of experiment or improvement, it is scarcely a matter

of surprise that the production of glass remained in a poor state both as a manufacture and as a philosophical problem. The same cause now no longer existing, a vast amount of progress has been made both in extensions of the application of this product, and also in the process of manufacture..."

Diverse opinions were expressed about both English and foreign design in glass. On the other hand the *Art Journal* wrote of cut crystal as being the highest state of glass art in which it thought English cutters excelled. Apsley Pellat, not suprisingly made similar comments in the notes to his company's display:

"The essential... qualities of good glass are ... its near resemblance to real crystal in its brilliant, ..refractive, and colourless transparency. In all these respects the productions of the British glasshouse are at present unrivalled."

In the opinion of the critic and social reformer John Ruskin, however:

"...all cut glass is barbarous, for the cutting conceals its ductility and confuses it with crystal. Also, all very neat, finished, and perfect form in glass is barbarous.."

Ruskin and William Morris main-tained a dislike of the practice of cut-glass preferring the more direct plastic forms of free-blown glass. Both critics praised Venetian glass because it represented the virtues of simple and honest craftsmanship. But it is difficult to imagine exactly what examples of Venetian glass Ruskin had in mind when writing:

"Our modern glass is exquisitely clear in its substance, true in its form, accurate in its cutting. We are proud of this. We ought to be ashamed of it. The old Venice glass was muddy, inaccurate in all its forms, and clumsily cut if at all. And the old Venetian was justly proud of it. For there is this difference between the English and the Venetian workman, that the former thinks only of accurately matching his patterns, getting his curves perfectly true and his edges perfectly sharp and becomes a mere machine for rounding curves and shaping edges, while the old Venetian cared not a whit whether his edges were sharp or not, but he invented a new design for every glass he made, and never moulded a handle or a lip without a new fancy in it."

Much of what Ruskin says about Venetian glass and glass-making practice is quite simply wrong. He had ample opportunity to examine the glass in both 17th-century paintings and first hand at the Felix Slade collection, shown in London in 1850 and reviewed in the *Art Journal*. Slade said his examples of the, *"...fragile products of the Venetian Glass Works..."*, were attractive to him for, *"...their beauty and elegance of form..."* Ruskin was not so much concerned with authenticity as with effect. His purpose was to promote a more honest use of the plastic qualities inherent in molten glass:

"The workman has not done his duty and is not working on safe principles, unless he even so far honours the materials with which he is working ... as to bring out ... their peculiar qualities...its ductility when heated and its transparency when cold.... All work in glass is bad which does not proclaim one or other of these qualities."

It is obvious that Ruskin's comments are based on a much deeper concern than mere aesthetic values. He stands at the beginning of a powerful reforming movement that set itself against the relentless tide of industrialization. Followers of the Arts and Crafts movement condemned the conditions most people had to live and work in. Ruskin and his followers held the view that beauty and creativity existed naturally in all men, at all social levels. All that was needed to bring them out was training and the provision of a pleasing and stimulating environment for work, rest and play. They saw design as means of tapping that cultural resource. Like other reformers they held up a vision of a new life and the products of their workshops were exemplars of that belief. To all but a small section of middle class intellectuals their radical ideals were at worst considered a heresy and at best irritating.

Though one of the prime objects of the reforms of the Arts and Crafts movement was to democratize the whole creative process from invention to consumption, their handcrafted wares were only of interest to their own aesthetic milieu. In any event the high costs of their craft manufacture priced their goods out of the reach of all but those who could afford to indulge in the romance of rural life whilst avoiding the realities of its many hardships.

The interest shown in Venetian glass by manufacturers was much more prosaic than the high moral stance of the Arts and Crafts movement. Venetian techniques like millefiori and ice-glass, described by Pellat in his *Curiosities of Glassmaking*, were taken up merely to decorate typical English forms and add yet more variety to the range of products.

Throughout the 1850s examples of Venetian glass were aquired by museums. The South Kensington Museum bought Venetian glass from the Bernal collection in 1855 and the Soulages collection in 1859. These obviously created much interest in thinly blown glass of a more fanciful form. Again the *Art Journal* did much to increase public awareness with its articles on the collections in 1858.

The Venetian glass industry, which had declined greatly in the 18th century was revived during the 1830s. The revival seems to have been part of a world wide revival in Venetian glass which is rather difficult to explain. Coinciding with its re-introduction in Venice the method of incorporating white threads in glass, called 'latticino' by 19th-century manufacturers, was being used in Bohemia at the Harrach glassworks, by George Bontemps in Paris, and Apsley Pellat in London. In 1859 one of the originators of the revival, Lorenzo Radi went into partnership with Antonio Salviati. They exhibited glass at the London International Exhibition of 1862 and in 1867 Sir Austen Layard entered into partnership with them. It is unclear to what extent this glass appealed to a wider market than antiquarian specialists but it certainly influenced other producers.

In 1868 Sir Charles Lock Eastlake, the President of the Royal Academy wrote a guide on design for householders called *Hints on Household Taste*. Eastlake, who like Ruskin and Morris disliked most cut and engraved glass, said of Salviati's glass,

"*...the smooth perfection and stereotyped neatness of ordinary English goods are neither aimed at nor found in this ware. But if fair colour, free grace of form, and artistic quality of material, constitute excellence in such manufacture, this is the best modern tableglass.*"

Engraved glass was a popular product throughout the 19th-century. By the time of the Great

Three decanters in thinly blown soda glass with blue trails by Salviati & Co., c.1902.

Engraved wine glasses in the classical style by James Powell & Sons, Whitefriars, c.1865.

Exhibition it was already beginning to supplant cut-glass as the favourite kind of glass on the home market. Cut-glass still dominated the export market. Throughout the 1850s and 1860s there was a revival of interest in classical forms and decoration. The slender classical forms and the subtle shading and line associated with engraving were ideally suited to the new thin blowing style. Similar classical influences are to be seen in the enamel painted wares and acid etched pieces of the period.

It was at the London International Exhibition of 1862 that the effects on design of this 19th century neo-classical revival were first seen. The engraved glass exhibited by Apsley Pellat was especially recommended by the *Art Journal* for its delicate patterns of Greek ornament using key, fret and anthemion motifs. It was at the same exhibition that

Engraved champagne glass made by the Birmingham glasshouse of George Bacchus & Co., c.1860. The influence of the fashion for the lighter Italian style is clearly evident in the stem.

CL. XXIV. 19.—VENETIAN GLASS. BACCHUS AND SONS, BIRMINGHAM.

A range of engraved glass in the Italian manner manufactured by Apsley Pellat & Co., from the catalogue to the 1862 exhibition.

fern-like patterns made their first public showing. The use of fern motifs shows how quick manufacturers were to seize on fashions. The public interest in ferns amounted to a craze with people seeking out as many varieties as they could cram into their homes.

The greatest influence on the development of British engraved glass, and indeed many other aspects of glass decoration was the influx of Bohemian craftsmen in the middle of the century. Without the presence of their superior technical knowledge and extraordinary skills the practice of engraving would not have reached the level of excellence seen in work exhibited at London. The craftsmen mostly settled in London, Edinburgh, Dublin, and the Stourbridge area. In London Paul Oppitz and Franz Eisert worked for prominent retailers of glass and ceramics including Copelands, Dobson and Pierce, and J.G. Green. Copelands supplied Oppitz with blanks made by the Stourbridge glasshouse of Thomas Webb which he then engraved to their requirements. His most famous, and best work, the Copeland vase, was designed by J. Jones. The largest number of Bohemian engravers settled in Scotland, including J.H.B. Miller whose workshop has been credited with the first examples of the fern decorations. The Bohemians were especially interested in naturalistic subjects and some of their most exciting work consists of pictorial scenes, such as landscapes and hunting scenes.

The decades following the Great Exhibition saw a number of highly inventive or innovative developments take place in the Midland's glass industry. One of the most significant for the production of good quality, yet cheap, decorated glass was the development of acid etching. The use of acid to etch a design, somewhat similar to expensive engraved glass, was discovered in Nuremburg in 1670 and the process was developed mostly as an adjunct to engraving and cutting. In England the commercial application of acid etching is credited to the Dudley glass-maker Thomas Hawkes working in the 1830s. Benjamin Richardson, who worked for Hawkes, introduced the technique at his Stourbridge works in the 1850s, and patented the use of India rubber for the purpose, which worked much better than the beeswax which had been used before.

John Northwood, a relative and former employee of Benjamin Richardson, opened up an etching plant in 1861. Here templates were used by low skilled workers to paint formal repeat patterns on glass freeing more skilled paintresses for the demands of naturalistic and figurative work which had to be done freehand. In 1862 Northwood, patented

a 'Template-etching Machine' which enabled him to use very cheap unskilled labour to produce decorative domestic table glass of an acceptable and consistent standard.

Manufacturers of pressed glass responded to the market's shift from cut-glass to engraved and etched glass by introducing designs of a lighter and more linear character. The use of naturalistic forms became increasingly popular in the 60s and whilst classical subject matter was never popular for pressed glass the use of motifs like the Greek key was common for borders. The American

Intaglio engraved jug by Alexander B. Miller for the firm of John Ford, Holyrood Glassworks, c.1880.

'lacy' style background of the 30s was introduced to fill in otherwise blank areas between these lighter patterns. A number of factories made domestic goods like candlesticks and butter-dishes in the form of classical columns and sarcophagi. Classical architectural details such as swaggs, lion masks, caryatids, and lions-claw feet were built into such humble wares as spill holders, jelly moulds, and cream jugs.

The re-discovery of the so called 'cameo glass' technique of Augustinian Rome was certainly one development in which Bohemian craftsmen played an essential role. The story of the development of English cameo glass starts in the 18th century with the Duke of Portland's purchase of an ancient Roman Masterpiece which was then called the Barberini vase. The vase became a benchmark of artistic and technological achievement. The Stourbridge glass-maker, Benjamin Richardson, who had acquired one of the jasper copies of it made by Josiah Wedgwood, offered a prize of a thousand pounds to the craftsman who could make an exact copy in glass using the ancient hand-carving technique. The first to take up the challenge were Philip Pargeter and his cousin John Northwood who was to execute the cameo-carved decoration. Northwood started to experiment with the Bohemian techniques of decorating

Jug with engraved silver deposit, c.1886. One of the many technological innovations introduced whilst John Northwood was Art Director.

cased glass – that is glass consisting of a layer of clear glass covered over with a layer of coloured glass through which the decoration was cut and engraved. 'Tag' engraving, as this intaglio style became known locally, was an important stage in the development of cameo carved glass. Intaglio engraving, in which the subject is carved into the thickness of the glass, is the reverse of cameo carving in which the background is cut back leaving the subject as a projecting relief. Northwood spent four years carving the Portland vase, and when completed in 1877 it was already famous.

Several pieces of cameo glass were shown at the Paris Exhibition of 1878. Northwood's achievements were represented by two pieces, the Milton Vase and the unfinished Pegasus Vase, commissioned by the firm of T.W. Webb. Cameo work was also displayed by Richardsons who employed the French engraver and medallist Alphonse Lecheveral. It is clear that these early pieces were made as 'state of the art' exhibits.

Joseph Leicester's report of the Paris Exhibition of 1878, which was published serially in *The Pottery and Glassware Trade Review* (*The Pottery Gazette*) said that there was very little evidence of naturalistic ornament. He complained that:

"...exhibits were adorned with battle scenes, figure piled upon figure, so overcrowded that the work appeared like dull stone. Wherever the observer turned he was met by the classical head, the classical form, the classical figure ....as if there were no room in the world for anything else but classical forms..."

He went on to suggest that floral motifs were better suited to the purpose of ornamenting glass objects.

The Paris Exhibition of 1878 also saw every historical style represented. Indeed, companies like Thomas Webb exhibited wares covering the whole range of styles – Assyrian, Egyptian, Persian, Chinese, Celtic, Mediaeval, Renaissance, etc.

Eclectic and exotic sources for designs had been used in Europe for many years. The French artisan, Philippe-Joseph Brocard, for instance, had exhibited glass based on Islamic, Renaissance, Gallo-Roman and Gothic styles in 1867. His designs, both for form and decoration, were based on painstaking research. This thorough approach to historicism was an important feature of his work and was to influence

'Pegasus' vase by John Northwood and Edwin Grice. It was exhibited unfinished at the Paris Exhibition 1878.

other French glassmakers, especially the young Emile Gallé. Artists and craftsmen went to extreme lengths to rediscover lost techniques they rightly believed were a measure of the excellence of former civilizations. By the 1870s the influence of Islamic enamelled glass was to be seen in the work of a number of European glasshouses. The Viennese designer Lobmeyer exhibited similar wares at the Paris Universal of 1878.

Other exotic cultures were making their mark on European taste in

the period. Following the expedition of the American Commodore Perry to Japan in 1859 trade between Japan and the West resumed again after centuries of isolation creating great public interest. At the London and Paris International Exhibitions of 1862 and 1867 Japanese bronzes, ivories, pottery, paintings, and carvings were a huge success. Even more than Islamic art the patterns and forms of Japanese and Chinese art were an exciting countercurrent to the dogged and continuous reworking of western historical motifs.

Brocard was himself lured by the novelty of Oriental aesthetics but seemed to find difficulty in transposing its sparce aesthetic into the rich pallette of his enamels. He had far greater success applying himself to producing enamelled decoration in styles much closer to his own cultural origins.

For artists and craftsmen of the next generation, who like Gallé exhibited at the Paris Internationale of 1878, the principles of paramount importance were those promulgated by Violet le Duc, such as truth to your material and the development of new styles rather than copying historical ones. The first sight of impressionist painting led many artisans to reconsider their use of colour and to turn to observing nature for ideas and inspiration. They adopted the more restrained yet fresher values found in

Japanese art.

Francois-Eugene Rousseau was among the early protagonists of the sparse aesthetic of Japanese art. Although he did not start designing until the 1870s his work was received with much excitement. The engravers Eugene and Alphonse Reyen placed his designs on forms made at the Clichy factory belonging to the Appert brothers. They too were influenced by the asymmetrical format of Japanese painting and ornament. His later work was made in collaboration with the Appert brothers developing new techniques and materials and at the Paris Universal of 1878 he exhibited a wholly original range of glass imitating the natural stones used for Japanese carvings. The natural veining and faults were obtained by embedding metallic oxides into the glass.

The early work of Gallé is very redolent of Brocard's enamelled pieces. Some items seem to be little more than exercises in the use of enamels and show little or no attempt at originality. Gallé, like Brocard, made careful studies of Islamic glass in museum collections. He was also much influenced by the exotic and sensual use of ornament and colour in the paintings of artists such as Delacroix and Manet.

The plastic use of glass seen in the exhibits of Rousseau encouraged Gallé to adopt a freer, more experimental approach to the manipulation of glass from the early 80s onwards. The technique of casing glass, first practised in France, as elsewhere, by Bohemian craftsmen had been used by Rousseau in the manufacture of glass blanks with inclusions.

Gallé's cameo glass, although using the full range of the Bohemian techniques employed in English cameo glass, derived its visual characteristics from very different sources and models. He was especially influenced by Chinese cameo glass of the Chuan L'ung period and the coloured wood block prints of the Japanese artists Hiroshige and Utamaro. Gallé saw examples of Chinese glass in the Brandt collection at the Kunstgewerbe Museum, Berlin, in 1884. He was especially attracted to their use of colour and asymmetry as well as their power to evoke mood in

Enamelled wine suite clearly influenced by a mix of Islamic and Venetian forms, c.1880.

the manner of poetry and music. His cameo glass of the 80s reflects these influences as he turns wholly to nature as a source of images and spiritual inspiration. In powerfully evocative works he combines natural motifs set in broad textured backgrounds with acid etched quotations from the work of poets like Baudelaire and Maeterlink.

The technique of 'marquetry en verre' was a much more hit and miss method of construction and decoration. It was a form of partial casing in which dabs of molten glass were embedded on the surface of the hot blown form. As with much of the art pottery produced in the period the concept of the fortuitous blemish played a dynamic part in the aesthetic appeal of such work. The resulting vessels were etched and carved as if from natural found material, adapting the design to suit the unique characteristics of the blank.

In the latter years of his life Gallé used appliqué techniques to produce some of his most exciting unique pieces. They were made by adding hot glass to the surface of the form, modelling whilst soft, and then refining it by wheel engraving. In some exceptional examples the additions were themselves almost independent three dimensional forms appearing to grip the surface rather than exist as part of it. By the turn of the century this category of his work had become wholly sculptural.

These complex and time consuming techniques were employed in producing works which although not always unique statements were nevertheless produced in limited and costly editions. They were made for a very small group of rich private patrons such as the Comte Robert de Montesquiou-Fezensac, an ardent collector of Art Nouveau, but were also bought by state institutions like the Musée Luxembourg and the South Kensington museums. By the late 1890s Gallé's work had been exhibited world-wide and began to exert an influence on attitudes to glass as a medium of expression.

In the mid-1880s Gallé set about producing glass for a wider market. In 1898 he said: "*I wanted to make art accessible in such a way as to prepare a less restricted number of people for more difficult works. I spread the feeling for nature, for the grace of flowers and the beauty of insects.*"

The technique of acid etching was ideally suited to the needs of mass-production and Gallé adapted his ideas so as to provide designs which could be easily understood by craftsmen working from written instructions and detailed drawings. From 1896 these pieces were also made under the supervision of Desire Christian at Bergun & Schwerer and were shown along with the more prestigious unique pieces at the Paris Universal exhibition of 1889. After Gallé's death in 1904, production of glass of this sort continued under the artistic direction of his son with little evidence of any change in design or technique. It is quite clear that most of the glass bearing the signature of Gallé was made and decorated according to his design and very rarely by the master himself.

The Ecole Nancy, under the leadership of Gallé, made a vital contribution to the revival of French decorative arts following the Franco-Prussian war. The renewal centered on Nancy led to the formation of l'Ecole de Nancy, Alliance Provinciale des Industries d'Art in 1901. A group of artists and craftsmen working in the Lorraine, including the glass-makers Daum, August Legras and d'Argental, held its first exhibition in 1903 at the Union Centrale des Arts Decoratifs.

Following Gallé's death the lead was taken over by the Daum brothers who produced glass employing all of his processes. They were very successful at the Paris Universal exhibition of 1900 though their achievement was somewhat overshadowed by the award of the Legion d'honneur to Gallé. Having produced domestic glasswares in variety of styles in the 1890s under the influence of Art Nouveau, their designs took on an increasingly organic and plastic character.

In 1906 the Frères Daum were joined by Almeric Walter who had studied at the Ecole de Sèvres where he learnt the technique of producing sculptures using moulded glass paste. The technique of 'pâte de verre' was re-discovered in the 1860s by Henri Cros who went on to work in the state-subsidised studios at Sèvres. Unlike Henri Cros, who produced one-off relief sculptures, Almeric Walter developed methods of repeat-producing his 'pâte de verre' wares. He used the lost wax method of casting and sectional moulds to 'cast' three-dimensional forms.

Despite having written an article in the *Review des Arts Decoratifs* in 1900 which condemned the tentacular style of many Art Nouveau objects, the work of Gallé and his followers in the Ecole Nancy was a major factor in the development of the new style of decorative art.

The development of Art Nouveau occurred as a conscious reaction against the heavy decoration and historicism of most 19th-century manufactured goods. The term derived from the name of a salon opened by Samuel Bing in 1895. Bing who had travelled in Japan and China as early as 1875 was a dealer in Far Eastern objects d'art and was responsible for exhibits shown at the Paris Internationale of 1878. He had already acted for Gallè by the time he opened his Maison l'Art Nouveau where, together with glass by Gallé, he sold work by Tiffany, Karl Koepping and the Daum brothers. His salon was reviewed in all the major journals on art and design — *The Studio*, *Kunsthandwerk*, *Dekorative Kunst*, *Art Decoratif*, and *Pan*. In general, the style is characterized by the use of a swaying curvilinear line moving restlessly over attenuated and twisted forms. In the early stages, forms and decoration were taken from nature rather than pattern books. Although it pretended above all else to be original it was in fact very dependent upon the historical precedents of Celtic, Norse and Japanese art forms.

The Arts and Crafts movement is more significant in glass manufacture for its effect on the decoration of glass than as a genre of design in its own right. Even by the end of the 1860s its criticism of English domestic glass, coupled with the revived interest in Venetian and light Roman forms, had brought about considerable change. In his *Hints on Household Taste*, Sir Charles Eastlake noted that in recent years:

"...people began to discover that the round and bulbous form of decanter was a more pleasant object to look at than the rigid outline of a pseudo-crystal pint pot carved and chopped about into unnecessary grooves and planes...For some years past the

forms of our goblets and water-bottles have been gradually improving; many artistic varieties of the material have appeared, and the style of decoration employed, especially with engraved glass, is very superior to what it used to be."

In 1874 James Powell & Sons commissioned the architect Thomas Jackson to design tableware in the plain style. His glass, like that designed by Philip Webb and later by James Powell's son Harry, illustrates the aesthetic principles laid down by

William Morris. The forms are simple and the metal, although transparent, is not of the same cold crystal clarity of cut-glass. The decoration, like the forms, is a truthful expression of the metal's ductility. These visual characteristics are exactly those found in Venetian glass.

This style of glass — a popular success at the Paris Internationale in 1878 — had many critics, not least within the more traditional sectors of the glass-making industry. Editorials and Letters published in *The Pottery and Glass Tradeware Review* during

Table glasses designed by Philip Webb in 1860 for William Morris and manufactured by James Powell & Sons who re-issued them in 1903. Their design was based on examples of glass seen in Dutch still-life paintings of the 17th century.

the 70s and 80s complained that such glass was 'flimsy' and 'inelegant'. Editorials of 1882, in celebrating the decline of aestheticism singles out the designs of Christopher Dresser:

"..The plain era in glass is dying out; plain wines and clarets as well as plain decanters are doomed, and the brilliant period is coming in again. At least let us hope that aestheticism is on the wane as far as glass is concerned for it means no labour, and as little trade, and certainly very little taste."

In 1888 Charles Ashbee, a follower of Ruskin and Morris founded the Guild of Handicrafts. The Guild, a co-operative of craftsmen working in woodwork, leatherwork, metalwork, and jewellery, exhibited at the Arts and Crafts exhibition of 1889. Unlike the Art-Workers Guild formed in 1883, primarily as a debating society with the aim of promoting unity in the applied arts, the Guild of Handicrafts was devised as a working co-operative. Although the influence of such associations on the design of glass cannot be demonstrated with reference to specific developments their ideas were of considerable importance to the development of design both in the UK and elsewhere. Ashbee's Guild was to be used as a model for similar ventures in Vienna, Munich, and

Dresden and they in their turn were to lead to the founding of the Bauhaus school of design.

Christopher Dresser's designs for table and ornamental glass share much in common with the work of Webb and Jackson and coincide with the aesthetic principles of Morris. However, unlike Morris, he did not adopt a principled and moral stance against industrial manufacture. He fully accepted the need to employ mechanical methods of production within the framework of division of labour. Morris promoted design by making it a natural consequence of production, centred upon traditional craft practice. Dresser, conversely, was much in advance of his time prac-

Claret jug and glasses in engraved crystal designed by Christopher Dresser, c.1880.

Below: A wide rimmed bowl in a marbled metal designed by Christopher Dresser, c.1885, illustrating the manner in which he exploits the ductility of the hot metal.

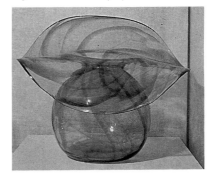

tising industrial design with fully formed ideas suited to the specific requirements of production and function. His work is close to that of the designers of the Vienna Secession.

Dresser, like them, believed good design placed truth to material and function above all considerations. In his *Principles of Decorative Design*, first published in 1873, he analyzed the fundamental requirements of the design and manufacture of glass saying that: "*..if the objects formed result from the easiest methods of working the material, and are such as perfectly answer the end proposed by their information, and are beautiful, nothing more can be expected of them.*"

Much of Dresser's glass, including a range called 'Clutha Glass', was produced by the Glasgow firm of James Couper & Sons. They later produced glass designed by George Walton, a member of the Glasgow School, the British equivalent of the Vienna Secession. Many of Dresser's forms are metaphors of natural forms and qualities derived from observation drawings. But he was also influenced by Islamic, Roman and Venetian blown glass. These influences can be seen in the bubbly metal and the use of trailed and pincered decoration.

As well as commissioning designs, both James and Harry Powell produced their own. Many of their ideas were taken not only from glass in museum collections but also from examples found in Dutch and Italian paintings of the 16th to 18th centuries. Amongst the pattern books and designs in the Whitefriars glasshouse archives botanical and herbal works have been discovered. New designs, based on these ideas, together with re-issues of glass designed by Phillip Webb and Thomas Jackson were produced at the turn of the century and their work had considerable success at the Paris Universale and again at the Arts and Crafts exhibition of 1903. In the wake of Art Nouveau there was a revival of interest in the delicate and lyrical forms of Venetian style glass. The trend received considerable impetus from the working display operated by Venetian glass-blowers at the Italian Exhibition at Earl's Court in 1904.

Throughout this period Stourbridge manufacturers continued to produce glass decorated by the cold techniques of cutting, engraving and etching which were so despised by Morris and his followers. Northwood's group of cameo carvers split

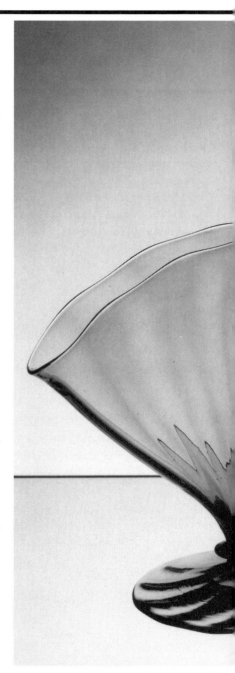

Part of a table service in the Venetian style make in a green soda glass by James Powell & Sons. Glass in this style was produced from c.1880 to c.1908.

up and by the mid-80s cameo glass was being made at the three major companies in the area, Thomas Webb, Stevens & Williams and Richardsons.

The brothers Thomas and George Woodhall joined the firm of Thomas Webb whilst still working for Northwood and in the last 15 years of the century they produced some of the best examples of English cameo glass. George excelled in figurative and landscape work of the sort used on vases depicting horse racing subjects and Scott's ill-fated Antartic expedition. The demand for cameo wares was so great by the mid-80s that quicker and cheaper means of making it had to be found. Commercial cameo glass relied very much more on the use of acid etching of simple floral subjects in a much thinner casing. The pieces were finished with detailed copper wheel engraving and except for their somewhat bland surfaces the overall effect was still one of skill and laborious effort.

In English glass manufacture, the influence of Eastern culture, especially of the Middle East and the Indian sub-continent manifested itself in several types of ware. In the 80s there was an increased use of floral motifs arranged in an asymmetrical manner. Special effects like 'verre de soie' (silk glass) and 'moss agate' were introduced by Northwood at Stevens & Williams. The influence of eastern aesthetics even found their way into cameo work. In 1887 Webb's patented a technique called 'ivory cameo' by which they sought to immitate some of the motifs and qualities of carved ivories. It was in a type of glass called 'rock crystal' ware that the influence was at its strongest.

In America, the designer Louis Comfort Tiffany, son of the silverware designer and manufacturer Charles L. Tiffany, was the single most important manufacturer of glass in the Art Nouveau style. Following a tour of Europe in 1865 Tiffany entered the New Jersey studio of George Innes where he trained as a painter. In 1868 following his success at the Paris Internationale, Charles L. Tiffany opened a showroom in England and Louis returned to Europe. Tiffany lived in Paris for two years studying under the painter Leon Bailly. In the company of Samuel Colman he travelled in Spain and North Africa. Later designs for glass were much influenced by the sinuous lines of the forms of Hispano-Moresque glass and the lustrous surfaces of excavated Roman glass.

In 1878, under the influence of Edward C. Moore and, much impressed by French decorative arts at the Paris Internationale, Tiffany embarked on his career in the applied arts. During his stay in Paris he became acquainted with the work and ideals of the English Arts and Crafts movement and in 1877 he and John la Farge founded the Society of American Artists. Tiffany started working in stained glass in the 1870s founding the Tiffany Glass Co. in 1885. The work was a natural extension of his design work in interiors and furnishings.

His glass was developed at the Heidt glasshouse and he personally undertook much experimental work with colour, opacity and lustre finishes. His first patent for a lustre glass, already a fairly well known process, was taken out in 1881. The process of subliming metallic salts onto the surface of glass had already been granted numerous patents of improvement when Tiffany made further application in 1886. This was for the much cheaper process of spraying metalic chlorides onto the hot surface of the glass. Tiffany's chief rival, Frederick Carder of Steuben Division, stated that the process was essential to the manufacture of inexpensive lustre glass. The process was quickly adopted by the manufacturers of glass, now called 'Carnival Glass'.

Tiffany's first attempts to make his own glass were interrupted when his glasshouse burned down. The fact that he employed the glass-blower Andrea Boldini of the Venetian factory of Mioti, suggests that he intended to make vessel glass. He eventually took over the Corona glasshouse in 1893, operated by Arther J. Nash a former glasshouse manager of the Stourbridge firm of Thomas Webb.

The qualities seen in Tiffany's 'Favrile' glass reveal his interest in natural forms and reflect the influence of glass seen on his various visits to Europe and North Africa. During a visit to the Paris Internationale of 1889 he saw an exhibition of Roman glass and was fascinated by the peculiar surface qualities. Many of the excavated objects had suffered from the corrosive effects of organic salts during burial. This left their surface pitted and gave them a coating of iridescent colours. On the same visit Tiffany made contact with Samuel Bing and engaged him as his sole European agent.

Tiffany products were always luxury items but a number of American manufacturers were making glass in a similar style by 1910. Like Tiffany, their home market was of greater commercial consequence, if less prestigious, than the European one. Of the many who followed Tiffany's lead, the most important were Frederick Carder of the Steuben Glassworks in Corning, Victor Durand at the Vineland Flint Glass Works in New Jersey, and Thomas Johnson at the Quezal Glass and Decorating Co. in Brooklyn. They

are considered by many to represent an American school of glass in the Art Nouveau style equal in importance to the Ecole de Nancy.

The earliest recorded use of a lustre finish on the very inexpensive wares manufactured in the pressed-glass factories pre-dates Tiffany's production of vessel glass. The English pressed-glass firms of Greener & Co. and Sowerby & Co. advertised irridescent glass in *The Pottery Gazette* and *Glassware Trade Review* as early as 1880. The first patent for lustre glass was taken out by Thomas Webb in 1877 for a range called 'Iris Glass'. Although irridescent glass was made by all pressed-glass firms in Britain by the end of the century, its manufacture never achieved the scale of the American factories where production on a vast scale started during the first decade of the 20th century reaching its peak in the late 1920s.

European manufacturers, like the American's, were much influenced by Tiffany's irridescent products. Under the directorship of Max von Ritter the German factory of Loetz started to produce what it called 'glaser à la Tiffany' from about 1880. The production of irridescent glass was probably a Bohemian invention. A patent for the technique was granted to the glassworks of J.G. Zahn of Solvakia in 1857 and irridescent glass was exhibited at the Vienna World

Fair of 1873 by Zahn and the Meyrs Neff glassworks. Unlike Tiffany's products, Loetz glass was mass-produced to bring it within the range of the popular market. Loetz products won several prizes at the Chicago World Fair of 1893 and the 1900 Paris Universale Exhibition.

In 1897 a group of Austrian artists and architects, later to be called the Secessionists, broke away from mainstream Art Nouveau as practised by fellow members of the Kunstlerhaus, many of whom taught at the Vienna's Kunstakademie. The Vienna Secession, lead by Gustav Klimt, Koloman Moser, Joseph Hoffman and J.M. Olbrich sought a national alternative to the curvilinear style common to international Art Nouveau. They believed the style had degenerated into a mode of decoration which for the most part was meretricious in its application and destructive of form. The following year they held the First Secession Exhibition in which they sought to:

"..bring to the Viennese public a general panorama of the life of the arts as it has unfolded during the last decade in artistic centres abroad."

Their desire to educate and inform public taste took its lead from the reformative notions of the English Arts and Crafts movement and, more especially Ashbee's Guild

Far left: Intaglio engraved cased glass, Bohemian, c.1855.

Top left: The 'Portland' vase. Cameo Glass by John Northwood for Benjamin Richardson, 1876.

Bottom left: The 'Homer' vase by Josiah Wedgwood, c.1790. This vase was the model for the form and lid of the 'Pegasus' vase.

Right: Bowl in a bubbly marbled metal with freely applied overlays, acid etched and designed by Emile Gallé, 1900. Gallé was very much influenced by the glass of Eugene Rousseau and by the work of the Symbolist artists.

Below: Emile Gallé, cameo carved and etched vase with quotation from the poet Maeterlinck, c.1900.

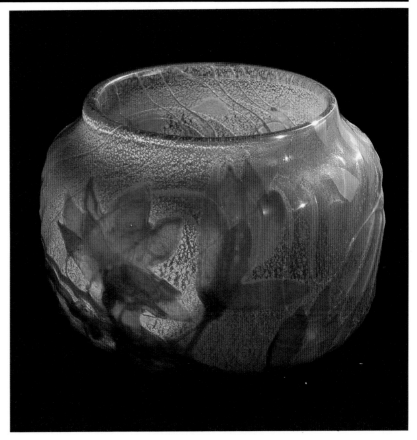

of Handicrafts on which they were to model there own association of studios. In 1902 Hoffman, in the company of the Director of the Kunstgewerbeschule, Baron von Myrbach, was sent to Britain by the Ministry of Education to make a close study of the art schools. Hoffmann visited Glasgow where he spent some time with Mackintosh and also visited Ashbee's Guild of Handicrafts.

The strong ties between the various strands of the Arts and Crafts movement and Vienna are very clear. Charles Ashbee and Walter Crane both became honorary members of the Secession along with Edward Burne-Jones. Work by Charles Ashbee and Charles Rennie Mackintosh was shown in the Secessionists' exhibition of 1900. Mackintosh's work was well known on the continent through articles in *The Studio* in

1897, following the 1896 Arts and Crafts exhibition, and in *Dekorative Kunst* in 1889. He exerted considerable influence upon the design of Moser and Hoffman. In 1900 Mackintosh was responsible for the Scottish section of the Secessionist exhibition and his contributions in the field of furniture design, illustrated in *Die Kunst*, were a sensation.

The intentions of the founders of the co-operative were summed up by the Secessionist art critic Hermann Bahr writing about the English Arts and Crafts movement in *Osterreichishe Volks-Zeitung* in 1899:

"..a great organisation to link art and craftsmanship..A tremendous studio, a colony of workshops where the artists will work with the craftsmen, teaching them and learning from them, craftsmanship growing from art,...organising the interaction between them, the connection between art and craft."

On this principle an association of studios called the Weiner Werkstätte, Produktiv-Gemeinschaft von Kunsthandwerken in Wien (The Viennese art-craft workshop co-operative in Vienna), was formed by Koloman Moser and Josef Hoffmann in 1903 and within two years employed over 100 craftsmen. Both men were Imperial Royal Professors at the Kinstgewerbeschule and were influential and prolific designers. In 1900 they were in Paris for the Internationale in which Austrian products were very successful and following which Hoffmann organized an exhibition of Secessionist decorative arts in Vienna. Koloman Moser described this Eighth Secession exhibition as being:

"..of prime importance in so far as artisitic craftsmanship in Vienna was concerned...One saw for the first time modern interiors arranged in accordance with a new Viennese taste..."

The designs exhibited by Moser and Hoffmann were described as being:

"..completely devoid of any ornamentation, elaboration and fussiness..nor is it in any case derivative..it is the direct expression of an individual personality, convincing, pleasing and unpretentious."

A.S. Levetus, writing on *Modern Decorative Art in Austria* in a special edition of *The Studio* 1906, said that:

"Professor Hoffmann's great aim is to follow in the footsteps of Ruskin and William Morris, to create a home of art in Vienna, and so bring a right feeling not only for the artist but for the craftsman who breathes life into the artist's work. Some of the artists trained at the Kunstgewerbeschule are employed by the Weiner Werkstätte; the seeds have been sown well, and from an artistic point of view, great success has been achieved."

Hoffmann, writing in the *Arbitesprogramm* (working programme) issued to visitors to the Weiner Werkstätte in 1905 expressed his ideas very clearly:

"The immeasurable harm caused in the realm of arts and crafts by shoddy mass production on the one hand, and mindless imitation of old styles on the other, has swept through the entire world...In most cases the machine has replaced the hand, and the businessman has taken the craftsman's place.

We wish to establish intimate contact between public, designer and craftsman, and to produce good, simple domestic requisites. We start from the purpose in hand, usefulness is our first requirement, and our strength has to lie in good proportions and materials well handled. We will seek to decorate, but without any compulsion to do so, and certainly not at any cost."

Even at this date, despite a clear realization of the needs of mass-manufacture, there was little intention of taking on the problems of industry.

"*May we also point out that even we are aware that a mass-produced article of a tolerable kind can be provided by means of a machine; it must, however, then bear the imprint of its method of manufacture. We do not regard it as our task to enter upon this area yet.*"

The Weiner Werkstätte did not possess the means to manufacture glass and most of its glass was manufactured in the Bohemian glasshouses of Johann Oertl & Co. Haida; Karl Schappel, Haida; Meyrs Neff; Ludvig Moser & Sohne, Karslbad; Johan Loetz Witwe, Klostermuhle. However, it was the retailing firm of

Vases and wine glasses designed by Koloman Moser for the retailing outlet of E. Bakalowitz & Son. Dekorative Kunst, *1901.*

Vase in opalescent glass, cased and etched and designed by Joseph Hoffman for Loetz, c.1910.

Irridescent 'Jack-in-the-pulpit' glass by L.C. Tiffany, c.1907.

Below: A range of irridescent glass — 'Aurene', designed by Frederick Carder for the Steuben Division of Corning Glass.

A range of irridescent glass by Loetz, c.1900.

E. Bakalowitz & Sohne that was to be the major commercial force in the promotion and distribution of glass of the Secessionist school. Later, and more tentatively, their rival J. & L. Lobmeyr became involved once the products had established themselves in the European market.

The first Secessionist glass was designed by Koloman Moser and shown at the fifth Secession in 1900. Moser's students at the Kunstgewerbeschule subsequently designed for Bakolowitz. From 1910 Joseph Hoffmann designed for J. & L. Lobmeyr in stark black and white designs on angular geometric forms. The decoration was produced in a new technique called 'Bronzite'. Hoffmann's students, Otto Preutscher and Michael Powolney, also produced designs for 'Bronzite' glass. The designs by Preutscher for drinking glasses were especially architectonic in form, decorated with simple geometric patterns cut through a coloured casing. The technique was very traditional but his

Table glass in bronzite designed by Joseph Hoffman for the Weiner Werkstätte, 1920s.

interpretation looked forward to the rationale of Modernism.

In Germany the first to follow the lead given by Moser and Hoffmann were Peter Behrens, Hermann Obrist, Bruno Paul, Bernhard Pankok and Richard Riemerschmid — co-founders of the Munchener Vereinigte Werkstätten fur Kunst im Handwerk (The Munich United Workshops for Art in Handwork) in 1898. This was followed by the Dresdener Werkstätten fur Handwerkunst, started by the designer and furniture maker Karl Schmidt. Mass-produced furniture designed by Bruno Paul was manufactured at Schmidt's factory in Dresden that year. Designers and craftsmen of all three workshop cooperatives were instrumental in the founding of the Deutsche Werkbund in 1907 in which the problems of designing for mass-manufacture were to be given first consideration.

Decorative stemmed glass with carved blue casing over crystal, c.1910.

3

THE
DECADES OF MODERNISM

1905-1940

IN reaction to the unimaginative historicism of most 19th-century manufacturers, the various reforming movements of the years spanning the turn of the century established the new aesthetic principles represented by the various aspects of Art Nouveau. For the most part, however, their products required the individual attention of craftsmen and constituted a small proportion of glass manufacture. In general terms, Art Nouveau glass was a luxury which, like so many present day 'designer label' goods were acquired for the status it conferred on the purchaser. By the end of the first decade of the new century the style was itself the subject of criticism.

None of the reforming movements did much to solve the universal problems created by the Industrial Revolution. The continued expansion of the mass-market and the resulting growth in mechanization demanded a technological as well as an ideological approach to the development of design theories and practice. The ideas articulated in the words and works of the followers of Morris and Ashbee, steeped though they were in the traditions of craft practice, proved to be of seminal importance to the development of Functionalism. The idea that there is a natural relationship between function and form was argued as early as 1757 by the French Neoclassical architect Laugier. The fundamental tenet of his beliefs was reiterated by Pugin, Ruskin and the American architect Louis H. Sullivan who, in 1895, made the much quoted observation that, '..form follows function'.

The search for a new aesthetic indentity able to embrace the needs of modern industrial society took a radical leap forward following the success of an exhibition of applied arts by members of the Dresden Deutsche Werkstätte in 1906. This led to the forming of the Deutsche Werkbund, its stated aim being: "*to provide a rallying point for the best representatives of art, industry, crafts and trades, and by their combined efforts raise the standard of industrial products.*"

In June 1907 Hermann Muthesius, a former state architect and authority on design, wrote a critical report on the state of design in Germany. In his report he blamed stagnation of the market on the poor design of manufactured goods. His opinions were shared by members of both the Munich and the Dresden Werkstätten together with some industrialists and politicians. In October, the Deutsche Werkbund was formed in Munich. Amongst the founding group were Peter Behrens, Josef Hoffmann, Josef Olbrich, Bruno Paul, Bernhard Pankok and Richard Riemerschmid.

Hoffmann, continuing as leader of the Weiner Werkstätte designed glass for Lobmeyr in typically graceful, blown-crystal forms. The firm of Moser of Karlsbad produced simple facet cut forms in coloured metal clearly pointing ahead to the chunky geometry of Art Deco forms. In these designs Hoffmann makes the most honest statements relying upon the inherent qualities of the metal, enhanced by very plain cutting which amplifies, rather than disguises, the formal logic of the forms.

Peter Behrens' work in the field of glass is typically simple relying on a straightforward combination of colour and form. The manner in which the components are formed and the means by which they are assembled is clear for all to see. There is no attempt to disguise the necessary joins of the construction by covering them over or inserting complex knops – additions to the stem. The forms of the drinking glasses produced by the Reinische Glashutten, based upon 17th-century forms, have simple bowls and very sturdy forms for the stem and foot.

Behrens became director of design for the German industrial group A.E.G. In 1909 he designed a new turbine factory in which some

A range of table-glass designed by Joseph Hoffman for the Weiner Werkstätte in 1915.

Facetted glass designed by Joseph Hoffman and made by Moser of Karlsbad, c.1920.

Tall glasses with simple, hollow, blown stems designed by Peter Behrens and made by Reinische Glashutten A.G., Koln-Erenfeld in 1901.

walls consisted of large areas of glass. His work influenced not only his pupil Walter Gropius, who made a similar architectural statement in 1914, but established a new approach to design in which the theory and the means of construction are exposed and form a major part of the statement. The use of entire walls of glass through which the construction and the functioning of the building were clearly visible became a leitmotif of Modernist architecture, explored more fully in the work of Le Corbusier and, more especially, the skyscraper structures designed by Mies van der Rohe.

The Great War brought almost all European glass manufacture, except that essential to the war-effort, to an abrupt, if temporary, halt. Some factories closed and many in the War zones were destroyed whilst others were turned over to the production of optical and scientific glass. Despite these temporary set-backs the War, although a useful historical marker, has no great significance in the history of glass. After the War most glasshouses returned to the manufacture of the sorts of glass their pre-war reputations rested on.

Following the cessation of hostilities, the Kungstgewerbeschule and the Hochschule für Bildende Kunst in Weimar were put under the directorship of Walter Gropius, formerly a pupil of Peter Behrens. In 1919 he merged the two institutions to form the Staaliches Bauhaus at Weimar. The stated aim of the new school was: *"..to co-ordinate all creative effort, to achieve in a new architecture the unification of all training in art and design. The ultimate, if distant, goal of the Bauhaus is the collective work of art, the Building, in which no barriers exist between the structural and decorative arts."*

The principles of the Bauhaus owed much to the ideas and activities of the Deutsche Werkbund and thereby the earlier aims of Arts and Crafts movements. The form of teaching adopted was based upon the apprenticeship system of the Craft Guilds by which the student associating with the master learned by example as well as by instruction. It was primarily through its new approach to the training of designers and craftsmen that the Bauhaus became the most influential school of design of this century. Amongst its early teachers were Lyonel Feininger, Johannes Itten, Paul Klee, Wassily Kandinsky and Laszlo Moholy-Nagy.

After the vehement attacks of the local Socialist Democratic Party the school, under the directorship of Mies van der Rohe, moved to Berlin in 1931. In 1933 the school's buildings were seized by the Nazis and closed. Endangered by the inevitable progress of the Nazi party and unable to preach and practise their truly democratic ideals the staff of the Bauhaus dispersed, many emigrating to America. In Chicago, in 1937, Moholy-Nagy opened the New Bauhaus (now called the Chicago Institute of Design). Mies van der Rohe became a professor at the Illinois Institute of Technology in Chicago. In 1938 the New York Museum of Modern Art mounted a retrospective exhibition of the work of the Bauhaus 1919–1928. Through its catalogue and the many articles and reviews the work and ideals of the Bauhaus were popularized as

never before.

In glass, the most prolific and successful exponent of Functionalism was Wilhelm Wagenfeld. At the end of the War he became a student of design and metalware at the Bremen School of Arts and Crafts whilst working for a local silversmith. Following this he attended the Drawing Academy at Hanau for two years before going to the Weimar Bauhaus in 1922 where he studied metalwork under Moholy-Nagy graduating as a silversmith in 1925.

On graduation he joined the Deutsche Werkbund and in 1926 started teaching at the Bauhaus. In 1929 he was appointed head of the department of metalwork and it was about this time that he started designing for the glass industry. His first designs, for mass-produced tea and coffee sets made by the Jena Glassworks in 1932 are very simple in form and undecorated. In the early 30s he also designed a range of heat-resistant oven-ware for the Schott glassworks. The forms, again of clean and simple lines, took into account both the limitations of machine-pressing and the requirements of domestic hygiene.

In 1935, Wagenfeld became Art Director of the Vereinigte Lausitzer Glaswerke for whom he designed many ranges of domestic utility wares and tableglass. His work included the 'Kubus' range of modu-

lar stacking containers and in 1938 the zig-zag shaped bottle for 'Pelikan Ink'. His designs for both the Jena Glassworks and the Vereinigte Lausitze Glassworks won prizes at the Paris Internationale of 1937 and were much publicized through editions of *Die Form* and *Kunst und Handwerk*. Wagenfeld was a regular contributor to such journals and wrote several articles on the topic of industrial design theory in which he stressed that function was a prerequisite of good design and not an end in itself.

The French glass industry was more seriously affected by the Great War than any other country's but many factories continued in production, turning to essential War work. Factories in eastern France suffered most (many being destroyed), and any shared enterprises with German factories naturally came to an end with the onset of hostilities. The Gallé company continued in production well beyond the War, despite Gallé's death on 1904. However, the loss of production facilities at Meissenthal, seriously affected it. Under the leadership of Gallé's son it lacked both drive and direction and held on too long to the ideas and aesthetic identity of its heyday in the 1890s.

During the 20s the work of French designers and craftsmen led the world in almost every area of the applied arts. French glass became a

byword for style and quality. The work of French manufacturers exhibited at the Paris Exposition Internationale des Arts Decoratifs et Industriels Modernes in 1925 carried off most of the major awards. The glass of René Lalique and Maurice Marinot played a vital role in popularizing Art Deco, the international style which derived its name from the exhibition.

As well as this new generation of designers some of those who had come to maturity as Art Nouveau designers, the Frères Daum, François

Decorchemont, Albert Dammouse and Georges Despret, responded to the changes in the aesthetic climate of the period producing some of their most exciting work.

The Daum brothers, Antonin and Auguste started producing art glass at the family glassworks in Nancy in the 1890s following their father's death. Until 1900 their work was very similar to Gallé's in both style and technique. They showed a new range of glass at the 1900 exhibition which, although very indebted to the symbolist style of Gallé, made use of

Following the lead given by Wagenfeld, other glass manufacturers started to produce heat resistant tea wares. This service was designed by Ladislav Sutnar for Schöne Stube, Prague 1931.

a new process. The technique consisted of embedding crushed and powdered glass into the soft surface of the gather. This enabled them to build up several layers of coloured textures. Glass made by similar means, called 'intercalaire' and 'ceramique de jade' attracted a lot of interest at the exhibition and the company put similar techniques into production on a larger scale. It is clear from such innovations that the Daums were engaged in many experiments with glass powders and pastes in an attempt to find different ways of treating surfaces in a direct manner without recourse to expensive cold work in the etching and cutting workshops.

The developments in 'pâte de verre' initiated by Henri Cros and brought to fruition in the work of the contemporaries Argy Rousseau, François Decorchemont and Georges Despret were well known to the Daums. They too were experimenting in 'pâte de verre' but do not appear to have produced any pieces. The commercial production of 'pâte de verre' started sometime in 1906 after the arrival of Almeric Walter.

Walter trained at the Ecole de Sèvres where the technique had originated. At Daum he headed a production team which included the Daum's chief technician, Henri Berge, who had been responsible for most of their experiments with the use of glass pastes. Walter's team successfully produced ornamental sculptures for interiors. His early designs are mostly for simple forms with reliefs of animal and vegetal motifs. After the War, during which they ceased production, they made larger three-dimensional works using part-moulds which enabled them to produce more complex forms. These later works reflect the monumentality and classicism of Art-Deco.

Following the War, Daum continued making Art Nouveau style glass for a while using the cameo carved processes. However, in the early 20s, ever sensitive to the slightest change in fashion they started to produce strong simple forms. These forms, often blown from transparent bubbled crystal were decorated in simple acid-etched patterns or very spare applications of applied trails. The clear, sometimes geometrical lines of their products of the late 20s suggest the influence of a new lead, René Lalique.

René Lalique was born at Ay in Marne in 1860 where he attended the Lycée Turgot. At the age of 16, an accomplished draughtsman, he was apprenticed to the goldsmith Louis Ancoc in Paris whilst attending the Ecole des Arts Decoratifs. In 1878 he studied silversmithing in England at the Sydenham Art School returning to Paris two years later to work for the jeweller Varenne. In the 80s he studied sculpture whilst working as a freelance designer of jewellery, wallpaper and fabrics. He became a friend of Samuel Bing whose Art Nouveau salon was his main outlet.

During the decades spanning the turn of the century Lalique became something of a cult figure in design with a distinguished and very rich clientèle. His patrons included the actress Sarah Bernhardt, the Rothschilds and later, Caloust Gulbenkian. In 1897 his reputation as one of France's leading Art Nouveau designers resulted in him being awarded the Legion d'Honeur.

In 1902 Lalique opened a small workshop at Clairfontaine where he employed four glass-makers to produce small glass objects and figures by the process of lost wax casting. These were exhibited at the Turin Exhibition and at the Agnew galleries in London. Because of his reputation such work, irrespective of its quality, commanded the attention of his milleu and galleries eager to display work with so famous a label.

The perfumer René Coty commissioned Lalique to re-design the graphics used to promote and label his products. As a result of this project, undertaken in 1907, Lalique came to redesign the bottles as well. Lalique's studio was not capable of making blown wares on a commercial scale and these first examples of his industrial design were made by the Parisian glasshouse of Legras & Co. In 1909 Lalique purchased the Verrerie de Combs-la-Ville and he was soon approached by other perfumers — Forvil, d'Orsay, Vijny, etc., and by 1912 he had ceased making jewellery and other artefacts and thereafter concentrated his efforts on the design and manufacture of glass. Lalique, unlike other designers of glass, gained practical experience in making glass and coupled with his knowledge of the lost wax techniques and materials used to produce detailed jewellery was to be of great importance in the next stage of his career following the closure of his glassworks in 1914.

Following the Armistice, Lalique purchased a full size industrial plant at Wingen-sur-Moder in the traditional glass-making region of the Lorraine. Despite the upheaval of the War the factory was a going concern and he was able to assemble a work force experienced in several aspects of manufacture. From the start, his intentions were to produce fine quality glass at a price the majority could afford. Wherever possible he used the mass-production techniques of pressing, centrifuge casting and mould blowing, but only if they could be employed without loss of standards in design or quality of production.

Lalique pioneered work in casting and developed the technique of spinning molten glass into the mould — centrifuge casting. This technique was used to make large, light shades and bowls with deep relief decoration of the sort used in the foyers of commercial and public buildings and the salons of ocean liners.

Two forms in pâte de verre by Argy Rousseau, 1920s.

Most of his small scale ornamental glass was made by a mixture of the usual pressing and mould-blowing techniques but done to a standard of finish much higher than was common with pressed glass of the period. Lalique was always careful to produce designs that made use of the advantages of production techniques without forcing them beyond the limits of what was possible.

The range of products made at Lalique's glassworks was greater than any other manufacturer could boast. He made car mascots, dressing table sets, tableware, lamp shades, ornamental sculptures, and a variety of household ornaments.

Maurice Marinot's glass was very different in style and ambition to that of Lalique though it was equally successful and influential on future generations of glass-makers. Marinot was born at Troyes in 1882 entering the Ecole des Beaux Arts in 1898 to

study painting and sculpture. In his 20s he was a minor member of a radical group of painters called Les Fauves, the wild beasts, exhibiting at the Salon d'Automne in 1905. The leading exponents of the style were Derain, Matisse, Vlaminck and Roualt. Their nick-name was given them because of their 'barbaric and naive' use of colour.

In 1911 Marinot visited the glasshouse of the Viard brothers near his family's estate at Bar-sur-Seine. Towards the end of his career he spoke of the excitement he felt watching the craftsmen work at the furnace, an excitement that endured throughout his life in glass-making.

His early work in glass consisted of enamel painting forms made to his requirements at the Viard works. Pieces decorated with bold motifs in stark colours were first exhibited at the Salon d'Automne in 1912. But from 1913 he started to fashion his own glass, an experience which was to lead to him abandoning enamel decoration by 1921 in favour of hot-work in glass.

In an article in *The Studio*, 1927, Marinot's ideas about the nature of glass-making as a mode of expression were clearly outlined:

"To be a glass-maker is to blow transparent matter by the side of a blinding furnace... to shape sensitive material into simple lines by a

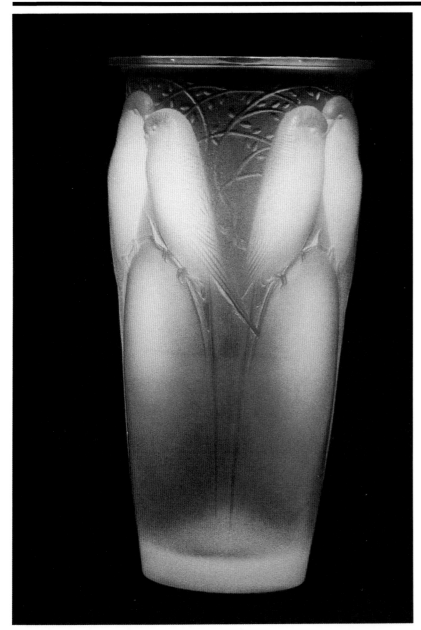

Above: Free blown vase in two layers with deep acid etching. Designed and made by Maurice Marinot, c.1932.

Below: A Maurice Marinot green bottle with acid etching used to produce a monumental carved surface.

A pressed glass vase with relief of birds made in opal glass, 'Ceylan' designed by Réné Lalique, c.1925.

rhythm suited to the very nature of glass, so as to rediscover later in the bright immobility of the ware the life which has breathed it into a fitting decorative form. This decorative form will be worthy of respect, or something more, as it bodies forth in proportion the two significant qualities of glass – transparency and lustre. I think that a good piece of glassware preserves, at its best, a form reflecting the human breath which has shaped it, and that its shape must be a moment in the life of the glass fixed in the instant of cooling."

In the 30s he worked alone with the aid of an assistant whose function was merely to fetch and carry additional gathers of glass. Marinot developed special glasses that worked at lower temperatures and 'froze' more slowly allowing him to produce truly massive forms constructed with very thick gathers superimposed one on the other. These forms were very exacting and required great skill in manipulation, as well as tremendous mental and physical effort. All of Marinot's work is very complex in structure consisting of several carefully worked layers with the most subtle changes in the quality of the metal. These qualities searched for in the hot state and frozen at the essential point of their maturity were later exposed by deep excavations of the surface using acid etching. In every respect the work is a plastic statement on the function of performance in relation to the perceived qualities of the material.

His work was widely known as a result of a number of exhibitions and innumerable articles not only in art and glass journals but also by critics of daily newspapers around the world. He regularly exhibited at world fairs as well as in specialist exhibitions in museums and art galleries. In Paris his work was on continuous display at Adrien Hebrand's gallery in the Rue Royale. In 1925 his work was exhibited at the New York Museum of Modern Art. At the height of his career in the 30s he was made the subject of a wider public. Although his work was necessarily priced beyond the means of all but the wealthy his vessels were much sought after by museums.

The glass he exhibited at the Paris Internationale of 1937 took the overall first prize in the glass section but was to be his last work in glass. The Viard brothers closed their glassworks that year. Marinot had worked himself to a physical standstill and after the Second World War which interrupted production of non-utility glass across Europe, Marinot returned to painting.

Scandinavia has been one of the most potent influences upon the development of 20th century design yet the term 'Scandinavian Design', was not applied as a stylistic label until the 1950s. At the beginning of the century there was little sense of regional unity. Two of the region's countries had yet to obtain political freedom. Norway was subject to Swedish rule and Finland, after some autonomy, was again under the direct rule of the Czars. The first two decades of the century witnessed the assertion of political independence and the strengthening of the regions' cultural ties. Their struggle for political freedom encouraged each country to explore their individual ethnic origins. Such interests gave birth to a popular intellectual movement which pervaded every sphere of artistic activity. National romanticism promoted a revival of the cultural traditions of folk-art and handicraft.

Even at the start of the century the strength of these cultural ties were pointed to in the review of Scandinavian products at the Paris Exhibition of 1900 which spoke of the ".. *powerful art movement forcing its way into the general art development of Europe..*"

Although outside developments left their impression upon the visual identity of the region, the romantic revival of the various strands of their cultural past played the most important part. Shortly before the end of the 19th century, following the influence of Rococo and neo-classical revivals seen elsewhere in Europe, there was a revival of traditional Viking forms. When the influence of Art Nouveau (which in Scandinavia was called the Jugendstil) began to make its mark on design it was grafted onto the stock motifs and symbols of the revived Viking traditions. Indeed, the acceptance of the new style was very patchy at first and in Norway it never took a firm hold. In Denmark it had little effect on the already high standards of design and craftsmanship of their own aesthetic movement.

The ideals expressed by Ruskin and Morris were well received in Scandinavia, although whether English ideology or design in any way directly affected design thinking in any of the Scandinavian countries cannot be demonstrated. The work and ideas of the Vienna Secession is very close to the rather restrained and geometrical tendencies of much Scandinavian design. This is not only true of those designs in which the interlace and stark linear patterns of Viking origins are to be seen it is also a characteristic of Denmark where the Viking revival was less vigorous.

The leading designers of glass in the period were Gunnar Wennerberg, Alf Wallander, and Anna and Ferdinand Boberg. Wennerberg's designs for Kosta Glassworks were mostly for cased and etched glass, resembling the simple two-tone work of Gallé. Alf Wallander and the Bobergs designed for the Reijmyer glasshouse, mostly using etched decoration on a clear or opalescent body. However, it is clear that such statements were in the minority. The Swedish Society of Arts journal, *Varia*, reporting on the Baltic Exhibition of 1914 said: "*Laboriously cut and gilded glass, with its form destroying reflections still dominates both ornamental and table wares. Simple forms with plain and harmonious surfaces are still very rarely seen.*"

Long after the decline of Art Nouveau, national Romanticism, fuelled by political and social reforms, continued to exert a strong influence on Scandinavian design. The Baltic Exhibition had been intended to serve as a showcase of Scandinavian abilities, even though only Denmark and Sweden were able

Bowl with applied lugs designed by Gunnar Wennerberg for Orrefors, c.1900.

Cameo carved bowl in green glass cased with yellow designed by Gunnar Wennerberg for Kosta Glassworks, c.1900.

to participate.

The Swedes found themselves out-classed in most fields. The Swedish Society of Industrial Design pressed glass manufacturers to employ Swedish artists to design their goods rather than copy foreign examples. By the time of the 1917 Home Exhibition at the Liljevalchs gallery in Stockholm this policy had been effected at the recently reorganized Orrefors glassworks.

The Orrefors glassworks, established in 1898 on the site of an old iron works, was acquired by Johann Ekman in 1913. Realising that its earlier products were of poor quality and out of touch with current market trends he appointed a new managing director, Albert Ahlin and set about reorganizing and improving production. He also approached the S.S.I.D. (Swedish Society of Industrial Designers) for help in finding an artist to improve the quality of design. As a result Simon Gate and Edward Hald were appointed. Both young men in their 30s and both of them trained painters.

Gate came from a farming background and studied at the Stockholm Academy 1905–9 as a painter and after graduating travelled widely in Europe working as a portrait painter. Hald, the son of an engineer studied painting in Copenhagen with Johan Rohde and then with Matisse in Paris in 1909 before going on to tour Italy. In addition to his work in glass, Hald also designed for the porcelain manufacturers Rorstrand and Karlskrona. The two designers' work was produced by the two most famous chairs of glass craftsmen in the region headed by the gaffers Knut and Gustaf Bergkvist.

It was with the help of Knut Bergkvist that Gate developed 'graal' glass, a form of cased glass in which the design is etched through a flash of colour and then cased over with a thicker layer of crystal. The design appears as a flat coloured pattern in the body of the glass. Examples of 'graal' glass designed by Gate, engraved crystal by Gate and Hald, and simple, blown utility glass with trails by Gate were on display both in the Home Exhibition and in the Nordiska department store in 1917. The utility glass and 'graal' glass were to be less popular abroad than their engraved glass.

At the Paris Exposition of 1925, Sweden, like Denmark, had its own pavilion and exhibited in the Grande Palais. Although Finland collaborated on some stands, neither Norway nor Iceland was represented. The engraved wares of Gate and Hald won several medals and Edvin Oller's work for the Reijmyer Glassworks, together with glass from Kosta designed by Lenart Nyblom and Karl Hulstrom, was also successful in winning a number of medals.

Hald and Gate worked in very different styles reflecting the difference

Intaglio carved vase by Simon Gate for Orrefors Glassworks, c.1925.

in their intellectual backgrounds and their different experience as painters. Gate, who had received the more formal training produced mostly detailed and heavily classical figurative subjects which were engraved using a deep intaglio style. His work tended to be used for commemorative wares and special commissions for presentation pieces to be given to foreign dignatories. Hald's designs are by contrast lighter in style and often whimsical and correspond more closely to what modern critics perceive as the Scandinavian style.

During the late 1920s the Functionalist ideals of the Bauhaus started to make a showing in all forms of Scandinavian design. The degree to which its influence was felt varied according to the country and the industry or craft. In Sweden it was particularly strong and especially in ceramics and glass. In Norway it influenced design at the Porsgrund porcelain factory and at the Hadelands Glassworks where glass of a Functionalist type was designed by Sverre Pettersen in 1927. In general terms the impact of Functionalism was very evident in the displays at the Stockholm Exhibition of 1930, particularly in the architecture and furniture on show. Although it was less apparent in the field of glass, the manner in which glass was used in the interiors left no doubt as to its aesthetic orientation. More important was

Above: Three crystal glasses engraved with figurative designs, designed by Simon Gate for Orrefors, c.1932.

Below: Decanter in crystal with engraved bands designed by Sverre Pettersen for Hadelands Glassworks, c.1930.

the effect that the exhibition was to have on future design policy and production.

At Orrefors around 1930, a new decorative technique called 'ariel' glass was developed from the 'graal' process but instead of trapping designs etched through coloured casings, the design is sandblasted onto a gather and then after re-heating another layer is cased over — trapping the air in the engraved design. These techniques were exploited in new ways in the 30s by another generation of designers working under the influence of the Modernist movement. In the work of Vicke Lindstrand, who joined Orrefors in 1929, decoration was of secondary importance to the qualities inherent in the glass itself. His work was heavier than previous Orrefors glass and this new monumental and clean style had an effect on the work of both Gate and Hald. Both designers started to produce 'graal' glasses with a very thick casing.

In the early 30s, steps were taken to improve the design of mass-produced glass. Finland's Karhula Glassworks organized a design competition for a range of pressed glass tableware. The prize was taken by Aino Alto for a water set with simple form, easy to use and keep clean. Her use of the material is both effective and expressive.

At the Paris Exhibition of 1937

Vicke Lindstrand, c.1930 for Orrefors Glassworks.

Scandinavian glass was again successful. Surface decoration had now given way to a simple architectonic use of forms in which the ductile qualities of the material in its hot state are exploited along with the limpid and refractive quality of high quality crystal metals. This new style is seen in the work of all designers of the late 1930s and is so consistent a theme as to suggest that it had become a characteristic of a style of glass that can be called Scandinavian.

In Sweden it is apparent in the designs of Vicke Lindstrand, Edvin Ohrstrom, Sven Palmqvist and Nils Landberg at Orrefors. At Kosta the same dedication to the natural qual-ities of the metal is seen in the work of Sven Skawonius, Elis Bergh and Gerda Stromberg.

In Finland the same Funtionalist values underlay the expressive use of glass in the designs of Gunnel Nymen, Artuu Brummer and Goran Hongell.

In America, although many glasshouses producing decorative wares closed for a while during the First World War, the glass industry enjoyed continuity of development until the Depression. In 1902, the Stourbridge Glass Co. of Corona, New York, founded by the English glass-maker Arthur Nash, was incorporated into the Tiffany Glass Co. and thereafter was known as Tiffany Furnaces. Tiffany Furnaces added many new products to the range of decorative glass issuing a number of variants of 'favrile' and new ranges of glass with internal lustre.

The company's market expanded greatly up to about 1913 and the period 1905 to 1919 was one of great experimentation, particularly with pieces featuring special effects achieved involving the use of multiple layers of glass, such as the 'Morning Glory' range. By the beginning of the Great War, public interest in Tiffany glass had begun to fall away and by 1920 the company was in financial difficulty and Tiffany appeared to lose interest in glass. In 1924 the com-pany was dissolved and the works continued under the name of A. Douglas Nash Co., producing similar wares until its closure in 1931.

Tiffany's former glass mixer, Martin Bach, founded the Quezal glasshouse of Brooklyn in 1918. Quezal produced many copies of Tiffany's lustre and 'favrile' glass. The Lustre Art Glass Co. also produced glass of the Tiffany kind in the early 20s.

Though Tiffany had many imitators and rivals, only Frederick Carder posed any real threat. In 1913, at the height of his success, Tiffany sued Carder for breach of patent rights when Carder brought out a range of lustre glass called 'Gold Aurene'. Carder, like many of Tiffany's technicians, had emigrated from England where he worked with lustre and similar effects long before Tiffany established his first glass-house.

Pressed glass waterset designed by Aino Aalto for Karhula glassworks 1932.

Carder had gone into partnership with Thomas G. Hawkes in 1903 to form the Steuben Glassworks in an old iron foundry at Corning, New York. Initially the company produced crystal and coloured blanks for Hawkes' glass cutting workshops. By 1904 Steuben was producing art glass designed and developed by Carder. In September 1904 Carder registered the trade name 'Aurene' for a range of lustre glasses, initially in gold or blue. The lustre effect was achieved by spraying the surface of the glass with metallic salts.

Unlike the Tiffany Furnaces, Steuben Glass stopped making non-essential glass during the War and in 1918 the Corning Glass Works acquired T.G. Hawkes & Co., including the Steuben Works. Carder was made Art Director of the Steuben Division of the Corning Glass Works. From that date the company specialized in the production of domestic ornamental and table wares.

Probably as a result of his training and experience Carder's designs were not tied down to any particular style. Steuben successfully marketed Art Nouveau glass but also produced glass in the Venetian style which enjoyed revivals both before and after the War. In the 1920s, he designed glass in almost every conceivable style. Between 1916 and 1923 he produced a range of glass called

Salad bowl set in cut lead crystal manufactured by T. G. Hawkes & Co., c.1895.

'Intarsia'. The technique involved casing a gather of crystal with a layer of coloured glass. A pattern was then etched through the colour. After re-warming the piece it was blown into a cover of crystal thereby sandwiching the pattern between the two layers. Both the technique and his designs were based upon earlier examples developed at the Orrefors glassworks.

Following the 1925 Paris Exposi-

Footed bowls and vases in intarsia glass by Frederick Carder, c.1928.

century with the discovery of natural gas. In the late 80s the Siemens gas-fired regenerative tank furnace was introduced and for the first time glass was fused in a continuous process. The use of gas also enabled more accurate temperature control throughout the manufacturing process. It was possible for glass to be fused, then fed to the moulds at the correct pressing temperature, before being fed into a tunnel oven where the finished wares were conveyed via gradually decreasing temperatures to the checking point.

Throughout the first decades of the new century, a number of patents

Vase using Carder's 'Cintra' technique, c.1920.

tion Internationale, at which French, Scandinavian, and German companies showing Modernist designs swept the board taking awards in almost every category — Carder's designs show similar influences. The French Art Deco glass represented by the work of Lalique, Frères Daum and Maurice Marinot was especially influential in the late 20s. Carder started experimenting with special hot-work effects and his range of 'Cintra' made use of Daum's and Marinot's effects achieved by rolling the hot gather over crushed glass embedding it into the surface. A casing of glass was then placed over the rough surface sandwiching the colour and small air bubble. Some pieces are acid etched with bold patterns in the manner Marinot employed in the

early 20s. No doubt influenced by the work of Lalique and Almeric Walter at Daum, Carder started to experiment with lost wax casting techniques and 'pâte de verre'. In the early 30s, Steuben's domestic wares ceased to be popular and the Division, no longer being profitable, was faced with closure by the Corning Directors.

Many of the products made by Tiffany and Carder were used as models for much cheaper wares produced in the mid-west by pressed glass manufacturers between 1907 and 1928. Several factors led to the production of pressed art glass in the Ohio basin. The region's glass industry, which had developed as a result of its large deposits of coal, expanded still further in the last decades of the for the automation of 'press and blow' bottle-making machines were issued. In 1903 M.J. Owens of the Libbey Glass Co. patented an automated bottle-making machine capable of making several pieces simultaneously. By 1905 glass containers were being made on fully automated machines continuously supplied from tank furnaces and by 1917 the full automation of pressed glass manufacture was made possible with the invention of a device to feed gobs of glass — measured amounts — into the pressing moulds.

Although full automation was

Pressed-glass punch bowl and cups with grape pattern in irridescent amethyst glass. Northwood Glass Co., West Virginia, c.1910.

important to the manufacture of containers and utility domestic glass the 'carnival glass' manufacturers did not use total automation, preferring to separate the main parts of the cycle. However, the semi-automation of manufacture coupled with the use of the hot-spray lustre process was essential to their growth in the 20s. Similar improvements in metal technologies also brought about improvements in mould design.

The Fenton Art Glass Co. introduced the first examples of pressed lustre glass. In common with the products of the other major producers it is only in the use of lustre that they resemble the work of Tiffany or his main rivals Carder and Quezal. The forms were generally crude and awkward with an over-use of decoration.

A contemporary of Frederick Carder, Harry Northwood, founded the Northwood Glass Co. in Wheeling in 1900. He started producing glass similar to Fenton's in 1908 and was followed in 1910 by the Imperial Glass Co., named after the Imperial Glassworks in Haida from which the owners had emigrated.

In addition to these major producers supplying 'nickle & dime' stores across the country, there were a host of small producers supplying mostly local needs. It was possible to buy a complete range of decorative ware, of about a dozen pieces, for less than a dollar. Such articles were often

Pressed tableware by Hazel Atlas Glass Co., Pittsburgh, c.1935.

given away as inducements by retailers of refrigerators and cookers. Their use as prizes in fairground sideshows and garden fêtes resulted in the nickname 'carnival glass', given by collectors in the 1950s.

It was in the manufacture of containers, especially bottles and preserving jars, that the developments in automated processes had their greatest effects. In 1904 the American glass container industry produced 12 million gross per annum which rose to 27 million gross by 1925. In 1920 the American industry led the world in container manufacture with exports worth in excess of three million dollars. The improvements in automated mass-manufacture of glass were of tremendous consequence to the development and success of heat-resistant kitchen wares.

In 1915, the Corning Glassworks produced Borosilicate (Pyrex) ovenwares using a variant of Owen's automated blowing machines, thereby setting a trend in kitchen wares which was quickly taken up by other manufacturers and grew into one of the largest markets in domestic glass. Utility glasswares increased considerably with the introduction of the refrigerator and the see-through oven

in the American kitchen in the 1920s and later. Glass was ideally suited to use in the kitchen because it was nonporous and transparent, and therefore easy to clean. In the sale of kitchen wares, hygiene became something of a gimmick used on every available opportunity in promotion literature and adverts. The success of pressed-glass in the kitchen and its comparitively low cost led to the manufacture of whole suites of matching utility and tablewares in the late 20s at a time of great

hardship in many homes.

The Steuben Division suffered greatly during the Depression as the middle market collapsed due to the state of the market and the proliferation of products, many of which now seemed out of date. In 1933 the

Drinking glasses in high grade lead crystal with teardrop knops.
Designed by Sidney Waugh, Steuben Division of Corning Glass, c.1939.

parent company, Corning Glass-works, decided to close the works but Amory Houghton Jnr, great-grandson of the founder of Corning, persuaded Corning's board to let him undertake an assessment of the Division's value and potential.

He proposed a new venture — a streamlined version of the old Steuben Division, specializing in domestic products made from their high quality crystal developed the previous year by Corning's chemists. Its purity and high refractive index were to be hallmarks of Steuben Glass.

Frederick Carder was moved sideways, though he continued to design and carried out prestigious research work in casting and 'pâte de verre' techniques. In the autumn a new company called Steuben Incorporated was formed with Corning Glass as the sole stockholder and Amory Houghton Jnr as Managing Director and the architect John Monteith Gates was appointed Director of Design, with Robert Leavy as Works Director in charge of production.

From the start, Houghton set about revising the relationship between design, marketing and production. He instituted a new design management policy and for the first time, design was no longer considered the sole providence of an Art Director developing ideas with the help of one or two craftsmen. The

Trumpet shaped table crystal designed by Sidney Waugh, Steuben Division of Corning Glass, c.1938.

new design team, led by the Director of Design included representatives from design, production, and sales. The top management structure consisted only of young men all keen to make their new project a great success. Houghton's first report to the board of Corning gives a clear indication of their attitude: "*We have a small group of skilful and experienced workmen, an extraordinarily pure crystal, let us take these, let us have a small amount of capital and a reasonable amount of time and we will attempt to make the finest glass the world has ever seen.*"

The New York Museum of Modern Art opened an Industrial design Department in 1933 which was to have a considerable influence on the progress of design in America. In its first exhibition of Machine Art in 1934, Corning Glass showed a range of Pyrex and the Steuben Division displayed glass designed by Frederick Carder and the industrial designer

Walter Teague. Teague, who had trained at a night school run by the Arts Students League in 1903, worked in graphics and packaging before turning to industrial design in the 1920s. In 1928 he was designing for Eastman Kodak and in 1933 designed the famous plastic 'Baby Brownie' camera.

In 1937 Steuben set up their head office and showrooms in Fifth Avenue and exhibited at the Paris Internationale with great success. Throughout the rest of the decade they expanded, opening showrooms in Boston, Chicago, Dallas, Detroit, Pittsburgh, San Francisco, and St Louis — cities representing new and old wealth. These showrooms, like the headquarters, were designed by Gates together with Sidney Waugh who he brought in to collaborate on design projects. Waugh had trained in the School of Architecture at the Massachusetts Institute of Technology and at the Ecole des Beaux Arts in Paris before joining Steuben in 1936. Together they developed forms and decoration which quickly established the reputation of Steuben Glass.

Design played a major role in the chief innovation introduced by the board of Steuben Glass; the development of a corporate image. Initially Gates and Waugh were responsbile for design, but the need for designers with an understanding of glass-making and the company's product

Water pitcher with a handle formed from two converging loops of crystal manufactured by Steuben Division of Corning Glass.

identity led to the opening of a design office in 1936. Trainees were sent to Corning to learn about manufacturing processes and gain experience of the material and then were sent out to the showrooms and on foreign study tours to develop a knowledge of the market. Steuben also adopted a very robust stance in advertising and promotion. In 1936 they launched a vigorous advertising campaign in Britain to promote the latest designs by Gate and Waugh mounting an exhibition of their work at the Fine Art Society rooms in Bond Street.

When Frederick Carder left Stourbridge in 1903 it was at a time of general depression for British trade in which the design of glass reached a low point. The poor state of trade and design was made even more obvious by the success of foreign manufacturers producing glass in the Art Nouveau style. Except for the designs of a few firms like H.J. Powell, James Couper, and James Ranken who exhibited at the Arts and Crafts exhibition that year, most British glass ignored the new style. They were still generally hostile to the sort of changes suggested by the Arts and Crafts movement and the Guild of Handicraft — ideas that were unacceptable alternatives to the status quo both for commercial reasons and because manufacturers were opposed to the political views from which such ideas sprang. Fol-

lowing the death of William Morris in 1896 the Arts and Crafts movement lost much of its impetus. Ashbee's Guild, unable and unwilling to respond to the real needs of an industrialized urban society, was put out to graze.

In the years preceding the outbreak of war, some British designers viewed the evolution of the Deutsche Werkbund with considerable interest. Some of them, former members of either the Arts and Crafts movement or Ashbee's Guild, recognized the philosophical parallels between developments in industrial Germany and their own society. Despite the War, or perhaps with some sense of urgency, the Design and Industries Association (DIA) was founded in 1915. An exhibition of German and Austrian manufactured goods was mounted by the Board of Trade with the purpose of demonstrating their superior quality of design compared to British goods. Manufacturers were informed of the need to follow the German example of employing trained designers and engineers so as to raise the standards of their products. The same year saw the formation of the Department of Glass Technology at Sheffield University followed by the foundation of the Society of Glass Technology the following year. These three institutions were to have a marked effect on the future of design and technology of

British glass.

Following the War, the Ministry of Reconstruction conducted an enquiry into the state of British design and published its report, *Art and Industry*, in 1919. On its recommendation a permanent venue and body for the exhibition of British design was established in 1920 — the British Institute of Industrial Art. The Federation of British Industry was also encouraged to promote design activity and formed an Industrial Design Committee. In 1924 it opened the first Register of Designers.

Several large circulation women's magazines promoted good design in the home as part of a more general desire to educate and improve society. They reflect the middle-class values of austerity and efficiency practised out of necessity in most homes and declared a public duty by the middle-classes themselves. Magazines like *Good Housekeeping* and *Ideal Home* carried articles on a number of issues affecting domestic propriety and in that sense the Victorian homily '*cleanliness is next to Godliness*' became enshrined in the belief that hygiene was the moral obligation of all classes of citizen.

Hygiene, function, and durability were values that played a major part in the design of products for the kitchen and was almost an essential ingredient in their promotion during the 20s and 30s. The adverts promoting the first new Pyrex imported from the Corning Glassworks stated: "*You will be amazed to see how much better every food cooked in Pyrex is....We guarantee it will not break. Buy your first dish today. It will last you a lifetime!*" The advert in *The Pottery and Glass Trade Review*, January 1922, also contained a visual comparison of the results obtained by baking bread in a normal loaf tin and a new Pyrex tin adding the footnote '*Pyrex bakes an inch higher*'.

The pressed glass manufacturer, A. Jobling and Co. Ltd of the Wear

Flint Glass Works, Sunderland purchased the rights to manufacture Pyrex in 1921. Initially they produced the Corning designs which had established the market but they soon had to develop new items to satisfy the requirements of English domestic traditions. Innovations in design were the province of the pattern maker in the mould-making shop. New designs were developed by modifying old patterns on the basis of marketing intelligence. Though

Above: Sherry set produced by James Powell & Sons in the 1930s. The simple bold forms are typical products of the new Wealdstone workshops.

Left: Casseroles in borosilicate glass: 'Pyrex'. James. A. Jobling & Co. Ltd, c.1924.

Right: 'Pyrex' kitchen wares of the early 1930s.

this was not always a recipe for good design it did at least ensure that the product satisfied the practical requirements of domesticity. By the mid-20s Jobling was making oven-to-table glass which boasted such advantages as: "*..adding charm to your table with its glistening transparency amid your silver and glass...*

Food retains its colour cooked in Pyrex..Your dishes will keep hotter than they did in those unsightly obsolete metal and earthenware dishes.' Although this advert in *Ideal Home* in 1927 is clearly aimed at a middle-class readership the claim that '*Pyrex saves labour because it washes up as easily as a cup*', would certainly not have been lost on the daily help. Jobling's products were amongst the exhibits of the Industrial Art for the Slender Purse held by the British Institute for Industrial Art in 1929 at the Victoria and Albert Museum.

During the 20s an alternative lifestyle was sought by a new generation of artists and craftsmen. For some it was little more than a nostalgic escape to the 'Good Life'. But attempts to give visual expression to the spiritual meaning of creative labour by craftsmen like the potter Bernard Leach and the graphic artists Eric Gill started a revival of interest in craft design of great consequence for the future of the applied arts in Britain. Under the influence of this 'ruralising' trend the Whitefriars glasshouse transferred to Wealdstone and thereby stepped even further away from the mainstream of industrial glass manufacture.

Some designers, equally sensitive to the diverse nature of their activity, felt as much at home whether designing and making one-off items or developing designs to be produced in

The 'Streamline' range of heat resistant wares manufactured by James A. Jobling. The form was introduced in the 1931. Centre: The colour sprayed version called 'Colourline' 1939. Left & right: 'Willow' pattern, 1939.

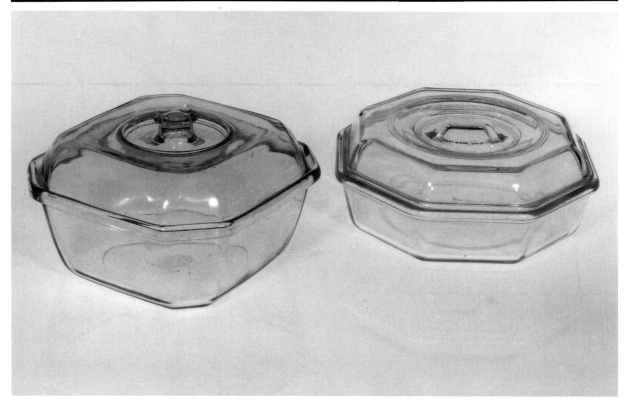

Left: 'Orlak' casserole designed by Harold Stabler for Chance Bros, Birmingham. Right: 'Phoenix' ware casserole designed by Raymond McGrath & Elizabeth Craig for the British Heat Resisting Co., c.1937.

their thousands by machines.

Harold Stabler, a founder of the DIA, trained as a wood-carver and metalworker at the Keswick School of Industrial Art. A follower of Ruskin and Morris, he was a regular Arts and Crafts exhibitor until the final exhibition of 1912. During the 20s, Stabler taught in the School of Design at the Royal College. His design work was very diverse, for in addition to producing individually crafted items in precious metal, he also designed mass-produced goods like tiles for the London underground and in the 1930s designed pressed glass for the Smethwick works and later for Jobling & Co. Thereafter Stabler, like so many others with handcraft backgrounds became more involved with indust-

rial production and in 1936 was appointed Designer to Industry by the Royal Society of Arts.

In 1930 he designed a range of heat resisting oven-to-tableware for Robert Chance Bros. The range, called 'Orlak', had clean geometric lines with recessed handles and like

Pressed 'Art Glassware' was also made on Wearside prior to the introduction of rationing. These examples were manufactured by James A. Jobling in 1937.

Jobling's 'Streamline' range was indebted to the pure forms and Functionalism of the European Modern movement. Chance manufactured the range from 1931–34.

Other companies had entered the market for heat resisting borosilicate wares. The aptly named British Heat Resisting Glass Co. of Bilston trading in the name 'Phoenix' also marketed a range of casseroles of octagonal form. In both cases the designs of the competing companies had lids with recessed knobs. Joblin's 'Streamline' range was a deep dish surmounted with a shallow dish which served the dual purpose of lid and serving dish. In 1934 Stabler redesigned Jobling's 'Streamline' range and followed the lead of the earlier design. Adverts for 'Streamline', like those of other companies in the period, stress the role of design. In an advertisement carried in the January issue of *Good Housekeeping* in 1936, the list of the product's virtues are a testament to the rôle of design:

"New! Sensible! Beautiful! Streamlined oven glassware! 'Pyrex' brand's newest creation! Casseroles with new, sweeping lines designed by Harold Stabler, one of England's

Left: Vase from the 'Pompeian' range manufactured by John Walsh Walsh of Birmingham, c.1930.

foremost industrial designers...new streamline handles not easily broken and ready to grip...their streamline shape makes them easier than ever to wash up."

Pyrex was not the only form of American pressed glass to be imported. Despite the success of English pressed decorative and table glass in the home market, cheap 'carnival glass' found a ready market in England. The only English firm to produce 'carnival glass' was Sowerby

of Gateshead. From about 1923 Sowerby made copies of the patterns produced by the Imperial Glassworks in either irridescent crystal, or blue, or amethyst. The popularity of irridescent pressed glass lasted well into the 30s and spread to other forms of glass manufacture.

In 1929 the Birmingham firm of John Walsh Walsh, whose main business was in cut or engraved crystal sought to extend their product range by introducing a new range of coloured glass called 'Pompeian' in which some pieces were given an

Compotes and dishes in the Venetian style. Glass of this kind enjoyed a revival in the 1930s and these were probably made by John Walsh Walsh in c. 1935.

irridescent finish. The earliest examples were made in either a blue or amber metal, infused with bubbles to give an antique quality. Walsh Walsh included 'Pompeian' on their stand at the 1929 British Industries Fair and Queen Mary selected a piece for purchase.

'Pompeian' glass was one of a number of examples of revival glass introduced by Midlands glasshouses like Stevens & Williams and Webb Corbett & Co. Walsh Walsh was the only firm to advertise blown irridescent glass, possibly in response to the interest shown in Venetian glass following the 1925 exhibition. Many people had reacted strongly against the Modernist trends in design towards the end of the decade and this may well have created a potential for revivals of forms associated with craft production.

It was during the 1930s that British designers began to organize themselves into a professional body. The process, having begun in the 20s, was set firmly on course by the founding of the Society of Industrial Artists in 1930. In 1935 the Royal Society of Artists organized an exhibition of British Art in Industry following which it established the award of Designer for Industry (RDI) of the Royal Society of Arts, as a means of raising the status of the profession within industry and commerce. The number of interested organizations grew during the 30s. The forerunner of the Council of Industrial Design, the Council for Art and Industry, was established at the behest of the Board of Trade in 1933. In 1937, the Council drew up a National Register of Industrial Art Designers which by the end of the decade listed nearly 30 designers of glass including Keith Murray and Clyne Farquharson.

One of the first designers to be granted the status RDI was Keith Murray for his work in ceramics and glass. Murray, who was born in New Zealand, trained as an architect at the Architectural Association School following war service. He visited Paris in 1925 where he saw glass from the Scandinavian and European glasshouses. He was impressed by the exceptional standard of continental design, especially in glass and ceramics, and was dismayed to find most British products were poor by comparison. On his return to England he began experimenting at the Whitefriars Glasshouse developing simple blown forms with engraved and shallow cut decoration.

In 1931, following the Swedish Exhibition in London, and possibly also due to enquiries by the Board of Trade into the standard of the design of British manufactured goods, the proprietor of Stevens & Williams set about finding a designer in the modern style with a knowledge of glass manufacture. Hubert Williams-Thomas sought advice from two of the leading exponents of modern design, Ambrose Heal and Gordon Russell. Russell had, himself worked with Whitefriars and Murray's services were retained on his advice. In September 1932 Stevens & Williams held an exhibition of prototypes of Murray's work in their London showrooms. An article on Modern Design in *The Pottery Gazette and Glass Trade Review* said that: "..attention has been concentrated on design in such a way as to break with convention but not with tradition." It was intended to run for 10 days but it was so popular it had to be extended for several weeks. In 1932 Murray was retained as a designer. His designs, mostly for table glass or vases, reflect the disciplined nature of his training. The forms are crisply stated, achieving a logical balance between volume and surface. Decoration, when used, is either in the form of engraved linear patterns which articulate the structural contour, or shallow cuts in simple repeats that measure out the surface in a steady tempo. Murray also made major contributions to the aesthetics of glass as well as the education of public taste through articles and public lectures. In 1933 he contributed a section on *The Design of Table Glass* in the DIA's (Design and Industries Association) information handbook *Design for Today* in which he set out the essentials of good design:

"The established purpose of the piece must be satisfied by its form...The form is all important; the profile, the mass, the weight, the colour...Decoration, if used at all, must be organized to express the form of the object not destroy it."

His glass, together with his work in ceramics produced by Wedgwood, played an important part in exhibitions at home and abroad.

The other major contributor to the design of English glass in the 30s is Clyne Farquharson. Not much is known about his origins and training, but the quality of his work suggests that he probably received a formal training in some aspect of design. His documented career in glass starts in 1935 with an engraved design called 'Arches' on glass, manufactured by John Walsh Walsh. In 1937 his work was exhibited at the Paris Internationale and appeared annually in the British Industries Fairs.

His ornament has the same carefully measured tempo and his forms a similar 'gravitas' to those seen in the work of Keith Murray. This is not to

Vase in 'Leaf cuts' pattern designed by Clyne Farquharson and made by John Walsh Walsh, 1939.

suggest that he worked in the same manner. Farquharson combined thin, rhythmical engraved lines with simple cuts of which the 'leaf' and 'kendal' patterns illustrated in adverts in *The Pottery Gazette* and *Glass Trade Review* were amongst Royal purchases at the British Industries Fair of 1939.

Farquharson continued to work at Walsh Walsh until its closure in 1951 when he transferred to Stevens & Williams, filling the gap left by Murray who resumed work as an architect after the War.

Other companies, following the lead given by Stevens & Williams, commissioned designs from leading artists of the day. Graham Sutherland, Paul Nash, Eric Ravilious, Dod Proctor and Dame Laura Knight all produced designs for work to be displayed by Stuart & Sons at the Royal Society of Art's British Art in Industry exhibition at Burlington House in 1935. Unlike Murray and Farquharson, they knew little or nothing about either the forming or decorative processes used and the DIA's reviewer in *Design for Today* cast doubts on the usefulness of such a venture in the industrial context.

Jug in 'Kendal' pattern designed by Clyne Farquharson and made by John Walsh Walsh, 1939.

4

GLASS IN
THE DESIGN AGE

FOLLOWING the apparent stand-still in domestic design in the early 40s, the first years of peacetime were taken up with the massive effort of establishing political, social and economic stability. The main task facing those glass manufacturers who had survived the interregnum was the change over from war-work to the production of domestic glass. British and American manufacturers faced a less daunting task than those of Europe, many of whom had to start over again. In retrospect this was to prove something of an advantage in the long term.

In Britain during the war-years, design had become one of the many weapons deployed to conserve scarce resources. The first Utility goods, pieces of furniture designed by Gordon Russell, were made in 1942. Russell was one of the first members of the Board of Trade's Advisory Committee on Utility furniture which had complete say over what may or may not be manufactured and therefore in some senses guided the course

Decanter and jug designed by William Wilson for Whitefriar's glass, c.1948.

of British design from 1942 until the end of rationing 10 years later.

The production of Utility wares had its origins in the spare aesthetics of the Modern style of the late 30s. In glass it is represented most notably by the pressed wares made at Jobling's Wearside factory. In 1939 they introduced a range of oven-to-table ware with sprayed-on colour. The 'Colourware' range in green, yellow, or blue, hardly had time to reach the shops before it was withdrawn due to "...the present emergency." They eventually withdrew all but Jobling's

plain cooking wares. The mainstay of Wearside's production during rationing was the aptly named 'Utility Streamline' range, first introduced in 1931. It replaced the later version designed by Stabler as well as their knobbed casseroles all of which used larger amounts of glass and more expensive moulds.

Advertisements published in the women's magazines throughout the 'emergency', highlight the advantages of hygiene and economy. In keeping with much of the editorial content of the period advertisements also encouraged the practice of home economics by providing recipes approved by the Ministry of Food. In these various ways Pyrex was seen to be 'doing its bit' to win the War.

The design of decorated table glass in the 50s, though not intentionally utilitarian was none the less still assessed in the frugal language of the Utility years as late as 1954. Describing a range of glass designed by Irene Stevens in 1949, but not manufactured until 1953 and then only for

A range of 'Utility' casseroles produced during the period of rationing, 1939–1953.

export, the Council of Industrial Design (CoID) said: "*Model 586: Made of colourless full-lead crystal. Functionally good, e.g. jug pours well, is well balanced. Tumbler is easy to hold. Fruit bowl is decorative when both empty and full. Simplicity in shape and decoration, and gives interesting shadow effects.*"

The CoID report on the state of visual education in 1946 condemned the traditional segregation of the arts and sciences but was even more critical of the low status given to non-academic subjects. In 1948 the new principal of the Royal College of Art (RCA), Robin Darwin, undertook a total re-appraisal of its aims and philosophy. He set out to develop the college as a place of training for future industrial designers and appointed practising designers and architects as its professors. These developments, together with the propaganda accompanying the Festival of Britain in 1951, did much to counter the criticisms at the time of

Glass exhibited by James Powell & Sons in the Festival of Britain 'Britain Can Make It' exhibition of 1951.

Cut crystal designed for Webb Corbett Ltd, Stourbridge, by Irene Stevens during rationing and not marketed until 1953.

the Britain Can Make It exhibition — a title which only served to highlight the fact that for most, the satirical quip, *"Britain can't have it"* was closer to the truth.

Design became an important agent of improvement in the post-war planned economy. Under Gordon Russell's leadership the CoID was responsible for co-ordinating all design for the Festival, an example to all of what could be achieved through united effort. The value and power of design as both an agent and symbol of unification was again apparent at the coronation in 1953. These events all increased the status of design in the community and ensured the support of the establishment in the many future attempts to improve design standards.

The CoID magazine *Design*, first published in 1949, was an important vehicle for promoting design as well as providing informed comment on design standards. However the opening of the Design Centre in 1956 and the introduction of Design Centre Awards in 1957 were to have an even greater influence on producers and consumers alike. The effectiveness of the new training provided by the RCA was acknowledged by the success of former students in winning CoID awards.

Until the mid-60s the RCA, Foley College of Art at Stourbridge and Edinburgh College of Art, were the only institutions providing courses in design for glass. The department of industrial glass at the RCA was opened in 1937 but was of little importance until the reorganization of 1948. The department did not possess its own furnace and could only supplement formal design training with experience in enamelling, engraving and cutting. Students received their training in blowing at the Foley College where all the forms were made. The two environments provided ideal circumstances for the training of future designers to the industry. In London, students had the benefit of major collections of glass as well as stimulating exhibitions in both the fine arts and industrial arts. Stourbridge provided an industrial environment in which to test and assess their designs for production glass.

The RCA became the most important source of designers of British glass over the next 30 years. Both students and staff have designed for all leading manufacturers.

Whitefriars Glass Ltd, long associated with aesthetic reforms and the raising of design standards, has always played an important part in the training of design students. William Wilson, its most influential glass-maker/designer, joined James Powell & Sons in 1928 following the

The 'Colourline' range introduced by James A. Jobling in 1939 but immediately withdrawn due to War regulations.

firm's move to Wealdstone. A contemporary of Keith Murray, he later played a significant role in the revival of diamond-point engraving, and as managing director of Whitefriars Glass from 1950 to 1973, appointed George Baxter to the design staff.

Following his studies at Guildford School of Art in the late 40s Baxter entered the RCA in 1951 and was appointed to the staff of Whitefriars in 1954 where he produced a wide range of designs for both tablewares and ornamental

Inexpensive mass-produced glass by the Ravenhead Co., a division of United Glass Co. Simple forms ideally suited to machine production.

glass. Baxter introduced some very exciting designs for moulded glass based on the natural textures of tree-bark and seashells. In the 60s Whitefriars again co-operated with a New Zealand born designer. John Hutton, perhaps the best engraver and etcher of glass in contemporary times, acid-etched a series of vases with motifs taken from his designs for the west window of Coventry Cathedral. Wilson was also involved in work by the other co-reviver of stipple engraving, Laurence Whistler, for whom Whitefriars produced forms to his exact requirements.

In 1945 United Glass Bottle Manufactures (UGBM), the makers of Ravenhead and Sherdley glass, decided to get off to a fresh start by developing new ranges of domes-

tic table glass. On the advice of the CoID they commissioned A.H. Williamson, a lecturer in the Department of industrial glass at the RCA. The employment of a qualified designer represented a major change in policy for the company. Previously new products were formulated on the basis of consultation between directors and customers. Williamson consulted with technical and production staff at UGBM and their distributors Johnsen & Jorgensen Flint Glass Ltd.

Design magazine in 1952 listed the advantages of the company's new policy:

"It seems evident that this close interest in design policy, taken at board level in each firm, is the most important factor in ensuring that the design standard of Sherdley and Ravenhead products is maintained. The results show what large-scale production can do to supply objects of good design, which at the same

Table glass designed by Irene Stevens for Webb Corbett Ltd, 1954.

time can satisfy the practical needs of the hotel industry and the home. The process ensures a finished product that is both hard-wearing and cheap with the advantage over hand-made glasses that the shapes and sizes are of a guaranteed standard. Although machine-made this glassware has a simple and clean appearance suited

When rationing was suspended, manufacturers returned to the production of cut and engraved lead crystal — a staple of the home market. 'Bouquet' range of cut glass designed by L. Green for Webb Corbett Ltd, 1958.

to the method of manufacture and is in no way an imitation of the hand-made article."

This managed approach to design became a feature of most mass-produced glass in the post-war period. All of the new ranges introduced by pressed glass firms were designed by consultant designers. The Smethwick firm of W.E. Chance & Co. Ltd (GB) commissioned Lady Margaret Casson who produced a number of designs for water sets and buffet wares like 'Night Sky'.

In the late 50s and throughout the 60s a small group of designers, all associated with the Royal College, made major contributions to the output of the four main glass manufacturers in the Stourbridge area.

'Royalty' range of cut glass with Georgian fluting designed by Tom Jones for Stevens & Williams Ltd, 1946 and produced in the 1950s. Presented to Her Royal Highness Princess Elizabeth.

Irene Stevens who tutored many Royal College students at the Foley College was formerly a designer with Webb Corbett whom she joined in 1946. Her designs in the 50s, like those of L. Green for a range called 'Bouquet' seem very indebted to the work of Clyne Farquharson then working for Stevens & Williams.

At Stevens & Williams, following the departure of Farquharson, Tom Jones became their chief designer in 1956. His designs for tablewares and drinking glasses are of robust form complemented by an economical use of cutting. This articulates the qualities of the metal and the skills of the cutter without resorting to complex prismatic effects.

Similar qualities are the hallmark of John Luxton's designs for Stuart & Sons. Luxton first trained at the Stourbridge School of Art from 1936–39. After the War he completed his studies at the Royal College from 1946–49.

David Hammond, who designed for Thomas Webb & Sons, also trained at the Stourbridge School of Art 1945–51 before going on to the Royal College in 1953–56.

David, Marquess of Queensberry, Professor of Ceramics and Glass at the Royal College, was retained as a consultant designer by Webb Corbett Glass in the early 60s. Lord Queensberry studied design at the Central School of Arts, ceramic

Wine glasses designed by F.H. Stuart and E.N. Khouri for Stuart & Sons, 1954. The simple straightforward design is a hallmark of the new generation of designers of the post-war period.

design and technology at the North Staffordshire College of Technology (now the North Staffordshire Polytechnic), and industrial ceramic design at the Royal College. Together with Martin Hunt, of the department of glass at the RCA, he formed the Queensberry-Hunt Design Group in 1964. Since 1965 he has also worked as a freelance designer for Rosenthal.

In 1963 Queensberry designed a new range of cut tableglass for Webb Corbett comprising tumblers, centrepieces, vases and bowls. The forms — called 'Queensberry' — are straight-sided cylinders with simple chamfered bases. Decorated with a regular diadem pattern named 'Harlequin' the range won a Duke of Edinburgh's Prize for Elegant Design in 1964. The stark geometrical form decorated in a repetitive and highly rational manner is characteristic of many Design Centre labelled products in the 60s. This somewhat logical solution of so-called 'design problems' was a feature of the quasi-scientific approach to problem solving adopted by the new professionals.

The final stage by which indust-

Above: Cut glass tumblers from the 'Queensberry — Harlequin' range designed by Lord Queensberry for Webb Corbett Ltd, 1963.

Below: Cut glass vases from the 'Bodiam' range designed by David Hammond for Thomas Webb & Sons, 1960s.

Above: Packaging became an essential part of the marketing of glass in the 1960s when total marketing concepts were developed. Illustrated is the 'Venetian' range of glass marketed by Ravenhead Ltd.

Below: A new concept in the retailing of domestic ware was spearheaded by Terence Conran in the 1960s. Packaging and catalogues emphasized the new 'designed' look, 1972.

rial design was professionalized followed the Coldstream Report on Art Education in 1961. Coldstream recommended that the National Diploma of Design be replaced by a degree-equivalent qualification. The introduction of the Diploma in Art and Design (DipAD) during the second half of the 60s changed the nature of design training and encouraged considerable growth of educational and career opportunities.

Running parallel with the development of professional design practices there was a proliferation of less enduring one-off design shops. They catered for a younger market seeking instant solutions to the many short lived fads in the 60s.

The simple, confident thrust of the early 60s, which pioneered what, in retrospect, could be called the Design Age was overtaken by more diverse trends. This evolution mirrored changes in social attitudes

'Victoria' wine service-designed by Frank Thrower for Dartington Glass in 1963.

which by the end of the decade saw young people asserting themselves *en masse* in a spate of differing convictions united by the single theme of protest.

Design in the 70s, the decade of protest, adopted a multitude of identities within the two broad themes of design by management and design by making. The Design Centre, which in the 60s mostly exhibited goods for the domestic habitat, showed an increasing number of designs for capital goods. In 1971, the Crafts

Storage jars designed by Frank Thrower for Dartington Glass in 1969. The very functional appearance of Dartington products followed the trend set by Scandinavian imports earlier in the decade.

Advisory Committee, forerunner of the Crafts Council, was established to promote and co-ordinate developments in the creative crafts. A number of exhibitions followed and by the end of the decade craft shops were to be found in every city and tourist centre. The different approaches to design were the subject of great debate in Polytechnic faculties of art and design.

In recognition of the many different aspects of design activity, the Design Council, formerly the CoID now makes awards in several categories of design. In more recent years the introduction of computer technology in industry and design education has begun to have an impact not only on the control and management of production but also on design thinking and implementation. The new technology has already begun to play a major role in the mass production of pressed-glass and mould-blown glass.

In the design of glass, as with many other areas of domestic product and craft design, Scandinavian designers were the world leaders in the post-

'Hartland' water jug and glasses, designed by Frank Thrower for Dartington Glass in 1971. Sets of stacking wares became very popular in the late 1960s following a lead set by continental designers like Tapio Wirkkala.

war period. In the 60s, especially in Britain and America, Scandinavian design was the benchmark of 'good design' to which both designers and consumers most often referred during the 50s and 60s.

The Second World War affected the countries of Scandinavia to differing degrees and in different ways. The development of design was naturally knocked off course but in all countries activities persisted and neutral Sweden provided a convenient window in which to display its continuation. At the end of the War their craft design was in a very healthy state enabling them to meet the demands of expansion head on.

Of the five countries, it was in Finland, Norway and Denmark that cultural development was most seriously disrupted by the War. Sweden and Iceland remained free, if somewhat isolated from their partners. Neutral Sweden retained a free press and its course of development in the arts was unrestricted if a little narrowed. It was to Swedish design that the other Scandinavian and most European countries looked for guidance after the War. Iceland, ringed in by the protection of Britain's western defences, was free but totally cut off from the mainland developments. During those five years her designers looked inwards, questioning their achievements and emerged with a stronger sense of indentity and a

more fully developed theory of design.

The 1950s was a time of consolidation in which design seemed to progress along a rational course. In the mid-50s the successes of Scandinavian designers at the Milan Triennale and the travelling exhibition Scandinavian Design did much to promote the concept of a regional style.

During the 60s, as in England, design became a professional activity linked to commercial enterprise and the furthering of corporate identities. It was also a period which, on the one hand, witnessed a return to the functional language of the Modernist era and on the other, a proliferation of designers working in an individual manner. In glass-making, the cult of the individual was most clearly expressed by one-off pieces of studio glass. At the beginning of the period designers like Sven Palmqvist and Tapio Wirkkala were already 'star designers'. *Design* magazine in 1952 described Wirkkala as: *"an outstanding and almost universal designer... already something of a national hero, the winner of several awards at the Triennale, and the first recipient of the rich Lunning Prize presented by the George Jensen Corporation of New York to the best Scandinavian designer of the year."*

Scandinavian design made its first real impact at the Milan Trien-

nale where Finland's stand, designed by Tapio Wirkkala, was awarded the greatest number of gold medals for both the stand and the products displayed. Glass was exhibited by the country's three greatest firms, Riihmaen Lasi Glassworks Riihimaki, Nuutajarvi-Notsjo Glass and Karhula-Iittala.

Gunnel Nymen designed for all three houses from the mid-30s till her death in 1948. She worked in both production glass and studio glass and in her unique pieces Nymen's style is characterized by a strong sense of form and the plastic nature of molten glass. Her production wares, mostly table glass, are always economical in form relying on a subtle articulation of mass and surface.

The designs of Wirkkala, Kaj Franck and Timo Sarpaneva have brought world wide distinction to the Karhula-Iittala glasshouse. They were to bring them annual harvests of awards in the 30 years since the War.

Tapio Wirkkala more than anyone in the past 30 years can justifiably claim to have been the single most influential designer of glass. He started designing for Iittala in 1947 and won three gold medals and the Grand Prix at the 51st Triennale. Through his work for the German company Rosenthal he has become a popular figure in the design of table glass. In the period following the War the designs of Wirkkala, like those of

Sven Palmqvist at the Swedish glass-works of Orrefors, reflected the return to the graceful lines of pre-functionalist glass. Though the influence was much more local than Art Nouveau, the principles of Functionalism still directed their response to the medium but their for-mal interpretations looked first to the natural environment for motifs rather than artificial construction. Wirkkala's exceptionally lyrical 'Chantrelles' vases, designed in 1947, in which he draws on the simple for-mations of funghi are amongst the most successful expression of such ideas.

'Chantrelle' vase designed by Tapio Wirkkala for Karhula-Iittala in 1947.

By contrast Wirkkala designed a range of stacking glasses in the mid-60s, a neo-functionalist response to the need to squeeze more into less. The idea reached back into Utility and had been used as a vehicle of effi-ciency and designed logic by desig-ners of catering wares in the 50s. In the 60's habitat it was one of a number of elements of the search for the ultimate in labour and space-saving environments. Its obvious benefits found favour with manufac-turer, retailer and consumer alike. Wirkkala's austere 'Karelia' suite was an instant success. A similar spare approach was adopted in the 50s at Nuutajarvi by Kaj Franck in his designs for simple cylindrical water sets with handleless jugs and by Saara Hopea for a range of nesting glasses. All of these designers also designed or produced unique pieces in which they used the material as a medium of expression — finding and developing qualities as the molten glass was worked. This mode of expression was to be of fundamental importance to developments in studio glass in America in the early 60s.

The designers Nils Landberg and

Sven Palmqvist, and Ingeborg Lundin of the Orrefors glassworks, were all gold medallists at the Milan Triennale of 1957. Palmqvist, who in 1954 had developed a new technique of forming glass bowls, was awarded the Grand Prix. The 'Fuga' bowls were formed by spinning molten glass into a centrifuge mould. The method was especially useful for forming large spherical forms. In addition to his technical inventiveness he was also a very resourceful designer working the metal in a variety of ways. In the 60s he produced delicately blown forms in pure crystal as well as the more familiar chunky forms of his 'Ravenna' series. By contrast his 'Light and Dark' wall for the Union Internationale des Telecommunications in Geneva constructed from blocks of 'Ravenna' glass and grey or white blocks of crystal is a sharply formulated design relying not only on the tonal interplay suggested by its title but also a stark dialogue between mass and surface texture and cold and warm colours. The idea was repeated for the Scandinavian Pavilion at Expo 67.

Nils Landberg, who like Palmqvist joined Orrefors in the 20s, trained and practised as an engraver before becoming a designer. In the 60s he produced tall glasses with delicately formed bowls drawn out into slender stems as well as studio pieces using similar manipulations of the

'Karelia' suite of glasses designed by Tapio Wirkkala for Karhula-Iittala in 1965.

metal to express its ductile qualities.

Ingeborg Lundin joined Orrefors in 1947. Her designs make full use of the glassblower's skills to produce subtle forms expressing the plasticity of the metal and exploring the qualities of Orrefor's high grade crystal. The blown 'Glass Apple' made to her design in 1965 is a wonderful statement of the organic relationship between performance and form in

blown work. Like a bubble it seems it could burst at any moment. This very precise balance of forces is an ever-present dynamic of her designs.

When Orrefors opened a new factory in October 1966 all three designers formed the bedrock of the new design activity. Gunnar Cyren who joined Orrefors in 1956, made a radical break with Orrefors' tradition for table and decorative wares in pure

Blown form in a bubbled metal by Kaj Frank for Arabia Glass, 1968.

undecorated forms and used the 'graal' technique to decorate wares with bold re-interpretations of folk-patterns which seemed to poke fun at their cultural origins. The 'Pop' range of glasses she introduced in 1967 captured the anti-establishment attitudes of the day. In contrast to these satirical revivals the designer Olle Alberius has returned to the 'language' and forms of the Modernist era at Orrefors and reinterpreted their values anew.

The Hadelands Glassworks continued production throughout the War with designs by Sverre Pettersen and Stale Kylingstad. In 1947 Willy Johansson became a designer working with his father, a gaffer in the factory. The Johanssons did much to extend and improve the quality of its tablewares after. At the Milan Trien-

nale of 1954 he was awarded a Diplome d'Honneur for glass which, as well as the tablewares, included coloured decorative glass in open textured glass shading from red to blue. Johansson was joined by Herman Bongard until 1955. His designs are chunky in form with linear inlays that describe the structure and mass of the form. Arne Jon Jutrem, who worked for Hadelands from 1950, exhibited with success at Milan. In the 50s Jutrem's forms were very liquid, full of movement in their undulating surfaces. He worked with inlayed trails and metal infused with bursts of bubbles which expanded and contracted with changes of form. Other pieces are more sculptural with grotesque additions of hot metal.

In Norway, as in Sweden, many designers in the 60s and 70s relinquished their posts in industry in order to satisfy more personal creative needs working on their own or joining with others to form craft cooperatives. Benny Motzfeldt, chief designer at Hadelands in the 60s gave up her post, eventually running her own studio in Frederikstad in the 70s.

Per Lutken, chief designer to the Danish firm of Holmegaard from 1942, continued the trend of Modernism established by his predecessor Jacob Bang. Bang's tablewares and decorative glass were solid, architectonic forms and were the sole representative of the style in Danish glass

just before the War. Lutken introduced major changes in style and policy in the 50s following a study tour of Italy at the time of the Triennale. He adopted fluid forms and the slightly coloured metal was sometimes etched to produce a soft satin-like texture making the external surface a more explicit statement of the form. Perhaps influenced by Italian glass, he used hot metal additions on already contorted shapes.

Jacob Bang returned to glass manufacture in 1955 at the Kastrup bottle factory. His early designs, considerably softer in form than his pre-war glass, were thinly blown

Footed glass from the 'Pop' range by Gunnar Cyren manufactured by Orrefors Glassworks in 1968.

Suite of bowls in current production at Holmegaards Glassworks.

in soft colour resembling the work of Konrad Habermeier at Gralglashutte. In 1965 the two companies merged to form the Kastrup & Holmegaards Glassworks at which Per Lutken was chief designer heading a large team making free-blown production glass.

Although its products only made public appearances from time to time in the world fairs and Triennale, the Czechoslovakian glass industry produced some of the most exciting and influential glass in the post-war era. Re-organization at this time got underway very quickly starting with the formation of the Centre for Folk Art Production which, after 1948, had responsibility for establishing a training programme for artists in industry. In 1948 the industry was nationalized and the many glassworks of greatly varying size and standard were combined to form more manageable units enabling the application of a planned development.

The programme of rationalization extended to the education of craftsmen and designers. The impor-

Bowls and wine glasses from Holmegaards Glassworks.

Glasses from the 'Mars' and 'Mercury' suites designed by Per Lutken. Holmegaards Glassworks, 1946.

tance of training a new generation was a necessity that was all too apparent in a society that had lost a large proportion of its young skilled men. The former trade school at Zelezny Brod together with the schools at Kamenicky Senov and Novy Bor, staf-

fed with new tutors, hastily set about training a new generation of craftsmen. The Prague School of Fine Art was raised to university status and under Professor Stipl the school of glass studies undertook the training of graduates in the design and production of blown and pressed wares. The programme of studies was revised from time to time in response to the changing needs of the national industry.

In the 40s the ability of the trade school to train craftsmen far outstripped the industry's ability to absorb them. Under the direction of the Ministry of Light Industry the reorganized industry set itself the task of rationalizing its activities. In doing

Wine glasses with knopped stems designed by Per Lutken. Holmegaards Glassworks, 1980s.

just that it became more efficient, needing fewer men and producing a more limited range of products. The Central Art Centre for Glass and Fine Ceramics was formed in 1952. It undertook a detailed survey of the industry, on the basis of which it was able to control the supply and demand of labour more effectively whilst at the same time encouraging diversification in design and production. Exhibitions of new products were organized locally and nationally to focus public attention on the achievements of their industry. The exhibitions were also used to educate public taste such as the exhibition of Art Glass held at the Museum of Industrial Art in Prague and an exhibition of the History of Bohemian Glass two years later.

Czech glass was seen at foreign exhibitors in the Milan Triennale of 1957 followed by the Brussels World Fair in 1958. Both exhibitions acted as a catalyst spurring designers and craftsmen to produce glass of the highest standard. Under the auspices of the Ministry of Culture, the Prague School of Applied Art and the Central Union of Czechoslovak Plastic Artists were responsible for organizing a massive programme of design and research and development for glass to be exhibited at international fairs. The project was a major boost to the development of all forms of Czech applied art but most especially

to glass manufacture. International exhibitions held in major cities throughout the world were also organized by the State.

Blown vase, acid etched and engraved. Designed by Jan Kotik and engraved by Cestmir Cejnar of the Novy Bor Glassworks, c.1960.

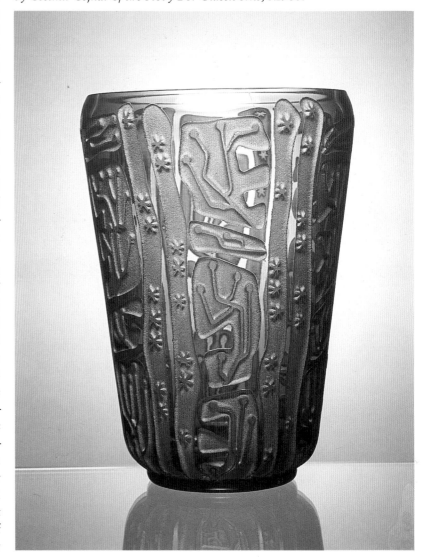

The range of wares shown at exhibitions from about 1958 is simply staggering. The effect of such glass on the international glass community has yet to be assessed and no doubt will require a thorough reappraisal of current views on the development of design in Scandinavia, Britain and America. The free blown forms of Jan Kotik and Rene Roubicek made at the Plastic Art Centre of the Novy Bor Glassworks and shown at the Brussels World Fair reveal a more advanced consciousness of the value of glass as an expressive medium than can be found in the work of any western artists. It was precisely this quality that was to be the prime concern of American pioneers of the Modern Studio Glass Movement.

Germany, with most of its industrial and commercial fabric destroyed and in a state of social and cultural torpor was faced with a mammoth task following the War. The late 40s were wholly taken up with reconstruction and rehabilitation. The enforced ideological schism in the east left not only the capital but also a number of major industrial plants on the wrong side of the border — a fate suffered by the Schott & Genossen Glassworks at Jenau. The joint efforts of Carl Zeiss, Ernst Abbe and Otto Schott had made the university town of Jenau a world leader in the production of optical glass earlier in the century. As a result of the growth in glass technology at Jenau its glass-makers were to become European leaders in the production of laboratory and domestic glass. The Jenau works produced utility wares in a both high-grade crystal and heat-resistant boro-silicate glass. Following the War these valuable skills were transferred to the west when the company reformed itself at the plant owned by the Vereinigte Lausitzer Glaswerke in Zweisel.

Design played a major role in the rehabilitation and development of Germany's post-war cultural identity. During the Third Reich, Germany set about irradicating all aspects of Modernism in the fine arts. The style was reviled and publicly attacked in special exhibitions of so called 'degenerate' art. There was a corresponding purge of modern forms in decorative glass, especially unique pieces. For economic reasons industrially produced glass, especially domestic glass of a utilitarian kind, was not affected.

Germany's leading designers of glass in the early post-war period were Wilhelm Wagenfeld and Heinz Loffelhardt. Wagenfeld, a designer

Heat resistant, borosilicate tea set designed by Heinz Loffelhardt and made by Schott & Genossen Glassworks, 1957.

for a range of industries became a Professor of Design in Berlin in 1947 but continued to design for both companies. Following the Berlin crisis he settled in Stuttgart and became a design consultant to the industrial giant Wurttemburgische Metallwarenfabrik (WMG) at Geislingen. His design workshop has been responsible for a number of major contributions in the field of industrial design including in-flight hospitality packs for Lufthansa, and porcelain for Rosenthal and lighting for WMG Wurttemburgische Metallwarenfabrik im Geislingen and for Schott & Genossen.

Loffelhardt, a student of Wilhelm Wagenfeld at the Vereinigte Lausitzer Glaswerke (VLG) in Zweisel in the 30s, returned to the company after the War. He was chief designer to both VLG and Schott & Genossen. When the latter moved to its new premises at Mainz in 1952 he continued as design consultant for their catering and lighting divisions. As designer to VLG he has been responsible for a number of suites of glasses for both domestic and catering use. Although quite ordinary in their appearance today, they were very innovative designs in the 50s and 60s.

The big success story of the post-war period in Germany is the glass and porcelain manufacturers Rosenthal-Porzellan. Philip Rosenthal had emigrated to America in the 1870s where he worked for a porcelain manufacturer. In the late 1870s his father's death brought him home to run the business and in 1879 he opened a porcelain decorating studio at Erkersreuth near Selb. Finding it increasingly difficult to obtain supplies of plain wares he opened his own factory at Selb in 1891. The company was very successful in the manufacture of wares in all styles prior to the Second World War and expanded into a large corporation by taking over a number of companies. Rosenthal gained a number of major awards including Grand Prix at Brussels in 1910 and Paris in 1937. In the post-war period these accolades have been added to at every venue for international design and the list of awards reads like a role of honour for the truly great designers of the 20th century. In the design of glasswares the list includes: Tapio Wirkkala and Timo Sarpaneva of Finland and the Danish designer Bjorn Wiinblad.

The success of the Scandinavian designers in the late 40s and early 50s, culminating in the stunning achievements of the Finns, especially Tapio Wirkkala and Timo Sarpaneva had a great impact on Philip Rosenthal Junior. He was already in the process of developing a new strategy for his company in which design was to play a major role in establishing a new identity and one that would place his company in the forefront of international design.

In 1954 Rosenthal started marketing its wares in in-store departments, an American marketing policy which enables greater control over the use of image and also ensures that the customer has the benefit of informed staff. However, in the early 60s the company introduced a totally new concept in design and marketing. At the Hanover trade fair of 1961 they launched 'Studio-Linie'. The press statement issued at the time explains the concept and identifies many of the principles of design and marketing policy which have led to the company's extraordinary success in the past two decades:

"With our Rosenthal 'Studio-Linie' it is our wish and intention to be publishers of what is good, that is to say, works of art which – irrespective of the school or movement of art from which they originate – are a product of our time and are also of a design which is both functional and suited to the materials from which they are made..only by offering products of genuinely high quality is it possible to induce the consumer to take an interest in 'dining culture' and set aside a greater proportion of his spending power for the purchase of products which come within this category."

All designs for 'Studio-Linie' are

submitted to a panel of judges, all personalities of international reputation in the field of art and design. The present panel of five judges includes figures as diverse as Lord Queensberry – designer and educator; Josine des Cressonnieres – Director of the Brussels Design Centre and General Secretary of the International Council of Societies of Industrial Design; and Heinz Spielmann – Keeper of Modern design at the Museum of Applied Arts, Hamburg. A number of Studio Houses for Contemporary Design have been opened since 1960 as showcases of Rosenthal products but also selling high quality design by other manufacturers of dining wares.

The Rosenthal Design Centre at Selb and the workshops of their glass factory at Amberg have not only been responsible for the development of some of the most exciting and advanced ideas in glass this century but they have also done so at a price within the reach of many householders. Their continuing support of new designers has done much to improve the standards of glass design and design education in other countries at the same time establishing

'Polaris' suite designed by Tapio Wirkkala for Rosenthal Studio Linie.

Above: Bowls and candleholders from the table suite 'Shape Without a Name', designed by Bjorn Wiinblad for Rosenthal Studio Linie.

Right: The 'Romance' suite of glass designed by Bjorn Wiinblad is part of one of the most popular ranges of tablewares produced by Rosenthal Studio Linie.

Rosenthal as one of the three major patrons of studies in glass together with Orrefors in Sweden and the Corning Glassworks in America.

The Austrian glass-maker and designer Claus Josef Riedel founded his own glassworks, the Tiroler Glashutte, in 1957 after working as a manager of a Neopolitan glassworks. His designs for Rosenthal, like those of his own glassworks, derive their beauty from an economical and effective use of the qualities of the metal. The 'Holdfast' range, mould blown with vertical cuts through the thick rippled body glass, are a true indication of his genius in applying very simple techniques to great effect. These qualities are also apparent in the very different designs for the 'Exquisite' range produced at his own glasshouse.

Riedel collaborated with Michael Boehm to produce the range of glass entitled 'Calyx'. The bowl of the glass is free-blown and added to the cast stem in which the feint mould lines become an element of the design expressing the graceful line of the petal forms.

Michael Boehm trained at the Hadamar School of Glassmaking of the Polytechnic of Applied Art in Kassel. He joined Rosenthal when he graduated in 1966. His designs of the past 20 years reveal him to be a very resourceful designer with a truly pre-digious talent for interpreting the qualities of glass in many ways. He has continually pushed the medium to the limits of its potential in a conscious effort to extend its possibilities as a vehicle for his designs. Unlike contemporary studio-glass makers he does not use glass as a primary medium of expression and the pieces made to his designs have great presence and character. The full range of his work for Rosenthal reveals Boehm's knowledge of traditional methods of working glass. The influences of the generation who trained him are equally apparent in the simple acceptance of truth to material, yet despite these various imprints the overriding statement is a personal one.

Wolf Karnagel, Professor of Design at the Berlin Academy of Fine Arts also designs for Rosenthal. He trained under Bodo Kapmann at the Academy of Fine Arts in Braunschweig. He has also worked as an associate designer at the Staatliche Porzellan-Manufacktur in Berlin. He has designed two ranges of glass for 'Studio-Linie', 'Joy', in 1969 and more recently 'Pandio'. The latter is reminiscent of the sort of strong and pure forms of many examples of Scandinavian glass in the 60s — qualities which have again become popular.

Possibly the greatest single-handed contribution made to the history of glass this century is that of the Dutch glassmaker Andries Copier. Copier started in glass as an apprentice in 1917 at the Leerdam Glassworks (NV Vereenigde Leerdam Glasfabriek), under Hendrik Berlag. Copier was awarded a silver medal at the 1925 Paris exhibition for the first of his 'Unica' series of glasses, followed with further success at the 1927 Stuggart exhibition. In the mid-30s the Leerdam Glassworks merged with NV Vereenigde to form the present company. The series of glasses continued after the Second World War and included designs by Floris Meydam, Sybren Valkema and Willem Heesen. Although it was in the 'Unica' pieces that Copier and his several colleagues produced Leerdam's most exciting and inventive pieces, the company's main product has been high quality table glass. The standard of design and the range of simple yet imaginative forms derives valuable influences from the more experimental work it underwrites.

The major contributions to Italian glass in the post-war period, as before, was made by the glasshouses of Murano. Designers and makers Paolo Venini, Ercole Barrovier and Giacomo Cappelin had all enjoyed success at the world fairs.

Venini, who was initially a partner with Cappelin, Vetri Soffiati Muranesi Cappelin-Venini & Co., established his own glasshouse after his success at the Paris International in 1925. In Italy, Modernism (Novecento) was interpreted in a more lively and novel manner than in northern Europe. Whereas in the north forms were arrived at by a care-

Tall, free-blown, stoppered bottle in blue and green by Paolo Venini in 1959. These forms became very popular in England and the USA in the 1960s and were copied by many companies.

ful and logical appraisal of the inherent qualities of glass, in Venice, 'truth to material' was the inevitable product of a craft in which free blowing and hot-glass decoration were traditional. Murano glassmakers all make traditional wares in gaudy ruby and gold alongside delightfully playful forms in bright colours. They have a long tradition of virtuosi production and also for major works.

Despite his own abilities as a glassmaker and designer, Paolo Venini made a practice of commissioning designs from freelance designers like Gio Ponti and Martinuzzi. In the 50s and 60s much use was made of highly colourful striped effects. The characteristic use of traditional methods of decoration such as 'vetro a fili' in which rods of coloured glass are embedded into the form to give stripes, are typical of Venini's work in the period. His work was a welcome relief amongst the serried ranks of stark northern forms. Some of his workshop's more audacious pieces, by Fulvio Bianconi, were made by kiln-forming sheets of glass into 'fazzoletti' forms. These, like his humorous figurines, were developed spontaneously through experiments with hot-glass techniques. Venini's own glass has the same fresh appearance of the design-by-making approach. Through exploring ideas in this direct way they achieved a vitality beyond the reach of most of

their northern contemporaries whose ideas were produced for them.

Above all else it is as individuals that most Venetian glassmakers have made their impression on the development of glass. The cult of the individual seems always to have been a distinguishing feature in a community that has a long tradition of applauding the achievements of the virtuoso. In the late 50s the community of glassworks provided vital evidence of the possibility of using glass not merely to give form to designs of the mind and drawing board but as a direct mode of expression. The use of glass as a primary, often exploratory medium was part of the tradition of Venetian artistry. In addition to the Venini works those of Barovier, Salviati, Seguso Vetri d'Arte and the Fratelli Toso and Moretti have each made different and important contributions to the development of the Venetian glass industry.

Ercole Barovier, like Venini, did much to revive the reputation of the Murano glasshouses in the late 20s. The processes he used relied mostly upon the use of subtle colour and open textures often reminiscent of Marinot's work. He and his son, Angelo, also produced vases and bottles of slender attenuated forms in 'vetro a fili' and in a bubbled, coloured glass with coloured inclusions. The surfaces achieved by Ercole were both harmonious and complex.

Carefully managed marvering over crushed coloured glass was used to great effect on strong pure forms – a process known as 'vetro gemmato'.

Left: 'Champagne Fountain' designed by Prof. Claus Riedel for Rosenthal Studio Linie.

Top right: Bottle from the 'Unica' range by Andries Copier, Leerdam, c.1935.

Bottom right: 'Papyrus' suite of glassware designed by Michael Boehm for Rosenthal Studio Linie.

Below: Decanter and whisky glasses from the range 'Holdfast' designed for Rosenthal Studio Linie by Prof.Claus Riedel.

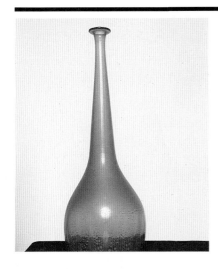

In the early post-war period he extended his earlier process and developed a technique of including small air bubbles in a controlled manner creating a view of texture – 'vetro rugiada'. Angelo Barovier's personal contribution to Venetian glass was perhaps greater than Venini's. A virtuoso of his art he has sought to express himself in the widest possible range of work. He has made especially exciting sculptures in which the plastic quality of the surface of the glass engages in an ever-changing dialogue with its internal characteristics as the pattern and mood of the ambient light changes.

The role of light in Venetian art was established as one of its unique qualities in the work of the painters Titian and Veronese in the 16th century. The light that affected them and the way it reacts in the watery environs of Venice is still a powerful and evocative influence on artists today. In the art of glass the Venetian glassmaker is a master of light.

The design of American glass in the early post-war reached something of a low ebb. Unlike Europe, into which America poured generous helpings of initiative and finance, the USA had little need to build a new world at home. The 50s was a decade of extreme conservatism for the generation that fought the War but one of rebellion for the next generation. Glass design reflects these changes in social and political attitude. In the 40s and 50s most companies produced very traditional wares. Cut glass manufacturers introduced richer cuts of rather massive form and gaudy in their effect. Pressed glass manufacturers like Anchor Hocking and Fenton Glass reissued some of their patterns from the pre-war years. Anchor Hocking's products went on to extend their designs to include glass with surface modelling in the form of split bamboo and also abstract textures. The Libbey

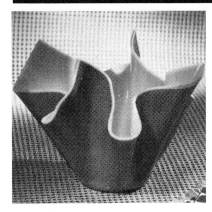

Above: A very poor imitation of Venini's work by glassmakers at the Birmingham firm of Robert Chance Bros, 1950s.

Left: 'Fazzoletti' form by Paolo Venini, 1954. A sheet of vetro à filli *glass was heated and then draped over a form and allowed to sag.*

Glass Co. of the Owens-Illinois Corporation, a major manufacturer of domestic glass, has made very cheap wares much influenced by Scandinavian glass exhibited in the 50s. Their 'Accent Stemware', one of its most successful ranges, was produced from the mid-60s. The glasses, which have very simple lines, are made in a smokey metal and represent the highest quality of design for fully automated production in the period. The companies Blenko Glass Co. and Tiffin Glass Co. have both produced free-blown glass of a good modern

design. Blenko made tall ribbed bottles expressing the soft plasticity of the molten metal. The Tiffin Glass Co., also a mass-manufacturer, in addition produces some fine craftsman-made table-glass in both traditional and contemporary designs.

Steuben Glass continued as the major manufacturer of quality glass after the War. By the 1950s Steuben Glass had gained an international reputation as manufacturers of crystal glass of the highest quality both in respect of the purity of its metal and the quality of its design. Some of the best designs spanning the War

are those of George Thompson. Thompson was a skilled designer of both domestic glass and rather more unique ornamental statements in which he interprets the qualities of his medium in lucid and strikingly lyrical forms. In addition to their reputation in manufacturing ornamental and useful domestic glass they were also famous for special pieces. Of particular importance in the advancement of Steuben's reputation were the unique commemorative pieces given by the State to foreign leaders and representatives. The best known example — 'Merry-Go-Round', presented to the then

Party style glasses decorated with bold epoxy resin decoration. Libbey Glass Co.

Princess Elizabeth by President Truman on the occasion of her marriage — was designed by Sidney Waugh.

In 1954 Steuben began commissioning designs from British artists,

Top left: 'Tawny Accent'. Machine blown table glass by Libbey Glass Co., early '60s.

Bottom left: A range of glass products from the glass houses of Murano, 1960s.

Below: Vase in heavy, free-blown crystal designed by George Thompson for the Steuben Division of the Corning Glass Works, 1959.

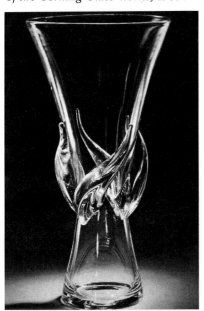

'British Artists in Glass'. Graham Sutherland, John Piper, Mathew Smith and the master engraver Laurence Whistler were amongst the first of many British artists to have their designs produced and exhibited around the world by Steuben.

The pioneering aspect of Corning's involvement has remained a continuing dynamic in the world development of glass. Not only in manufacture but, perhaps of greater consequence, since the 60s, also in the promotion of interest in the design of glass internationally and the study of its history. The Corning Institute is the world's most important contributor to the study of glass. The exhibitions of New Glass, starting in 1959, have provided a much needed critical forum for the work of designers and craftsmen in glass throughout the world.

Despite the popularity of the travelling exhibitions of Scandinavian design the response of American manufacturers lacked any real conviction or vitality. It did not fall within their tradition. American glass factories simply were not equipped to pursue production on the small scale of the Scandinavian houses. It was some time before they were able to respond by setting up studios within their vast automated plants.

The European practise of using glass as a medium of expression and not merely to make useful wares

began to affect American attitudes towards glass as can be seen in the policies of companies like Steuben. In the early 50s a young designer, Harvey Littleton, working in the so-called 'top of the oven shop' at Steuben was fully aware of such influences. He had already begun to give consideration to the possibilities of using glass as an expressive medium.

He and a small group of pioneers were to bring about the single most important development in the manufacture and design of glass since the introduction of pressed glass manufacture some 150 years earlier. The changes in the design and manufacture of glass affected the fundamental role of glass as a medium in the decorative arts. The evolution of glass as a vehicle of abstract expressionism within the domestic rather than public habitat has reshaped public attitudes towards glass in much the same way that studio pottery affected ceramics.

Harvey Littleton started his career as a sculptor at Cranbrook College, Michigan. The college was founded in 1930 by George Booth, an enthusiastic advocat of the principles of the English Arts and Crafts movement. It was staffed by a number of European refugee artists and craftsmen under the leadership of the Finnish architect and social reformer Eliel Saarinen.

Littleton's career was cut short by

the attack on Pearl Harbour and he found himself in a mobilization camp in England in 1942. Following the Victory in Europe he was stationed near Brighton where he attended pottery classes held by Nora Braden, a pupil of Bernard Leach. When he was demobbed in 1945 he was employed at the Corning Glassworks where his father was Chief Chemist. In 1946 he enrolled at Michigan University on a product design course and following graduation he again went to the Cranbrook Academy where he majored in the ceramics school under the Finnish potter Maija Grotell along with Peter Voulkos, Carlton Ball and Charles Lakofsky.

During this period Littleton taught part-time at the Toledo Museum of Art. After gaining his Masters degree in Fine Arts he took up a teaching post at the University of Wisconsin at Madison. He very quickly gained a national reputation for his work in design education and became a prominent member of the American Crafts Council as midwestern representative. It was in meetings of the council that he first advanced his ideas about solo work in hot glass.

In 1957 he took a sabbatical to study Hispano-Moresque pottery and was asked to do some research work on Spanish glass for the Corning Museum. Littleton also saw the President of the Steuben Division,

Arthur Houghton, and asked if he knew of anyone currently practising glassmaking in that manner. On his suggestion he sought out Jean Sela in Paris but he had ceased work in 1950. Sela suggested that he should go to Venice. Because the Murano glassmakers were typically very secretive he was forced to join the daytrippers' excursions to the demonstration workshops in the city of Venice. He found them using small furnaces at which two craftsmen worked independently except when needing help in collecting extra gathers of glass to add to the piece. Littleton took this information, together with drawings and some tools, back to the States.

He set about establishing a group of artists with a similar belief in glass as an expressive medium. He had by this time progressed beyond his initial desire to revive glassblowing by the individual. In Italy it was quite evident that that in itself did not result in unique activity. He was not interested in using glass as a susbstitute material for clay in manufacturing useful, albeit individual, items. Writing in *Glass Art* in 1974 Littleton said that glass:

"..did not, it seemed to me, have great potential as a production material — producing objects for use in the home, which was the philosophy that many of the artist/craftsmen pursued

...I was becoming increasingly disenchanted with that, especially as I saw the expressionistic pots of Peter Voulkos...which dominated the pottery of the late 50s."

At the 1959 conference of the ACC (American Crafts Council) held at Lake George, NY, a panel with special responsibility for furthering glass as an artistic medium was formed — Littleton, Paul Perrot of the Corning Institue, Michael and Francis Higgins of Chicago and Earl McCutcheon of the University of Georgia. This was followed by a paper on glassmaking for the ACC in late 1960. As a result Otto Whitman of the Toledo Museum of Art offered facilities and funds for the first practical seminar on glass.

Following initial failure to make a metal that would melt thoroughly they were joined by Dominick Labino, a retired technician and consultant on glass chemistry with a Glassfibre manufacturer. Having made the first pieces of solo hot-glass since the 1940s they were joined by a retired glass-blower from the Libbey Glass Co. in Toldeo and he became their first tutor.

The result of these experiments in the summer of 1962 was the formulation of a metal that would melt at low temperatures and the design of a cheap small furnace fuelled on bottled propane. Most important of all they had demonstrated that glass could be worked by an individual with a minimum of equipment.

After the project closed Littleton made a survey tour of Europe and England. He found that students were only taught design. Only at the Gottenborg Art School in Sweden and at the Foley College in Stourbridge did students actually get practical experience in working with glass. The standard practice elsewhere was for students to be tutored in the processes of manufacture and have a few pieces made in the industry if they were lucky.

When Littleton made his European survey he only found one artist working solo in hot-glass. Erwin Eisch of Frauenau in Bavaria had been experimenting with glass as a sculptural medium for about 18 months. He had held a one-man exhibition in Stuttgart in June 1962. Eisch's family had been engaged in glass manufacture for many years. He was trained to blow by his father and then attended the Trade Glassfachschule at Weissel where he trained as an engraver. He then attended the Academy of Art in Munich studying sculpture and interior design. It was the liberating experience of his studies within the School of Fine Arts that led him to condemn the trend in design education that had replaced creativity linked to manual experience with abstract design principles. Eisch says that as a result of his studies in sculpture with Professor Heinrich Kirchener:

"..the experience of three-dimensional form brought me out of the confined atmosphere of two-dimensional designing. The expression of the material shaped by the hands, the mind and the spirit – this brought me a great freedom and unfolding of the creative nature. I soon discovered that one does not discover new forms and ideas only in the conventional method of design – by drawing the designs."

Eisch was the most influential of the group in formulating the principle aesthetics of the New Wave Studio Glass movement. In 1963 the University of Wisconsin started the first studio-glass teaching programme. The first student of this programme to matriculate in glass was Marvin Lipofsky who went on to teach glassmaking at Berkely California. The most productive of the first group is Dominick Labino who having spent his life in the technology of glass found a new, second career. He continued to work in the early manner which was to create a form by experimenting with the material on the iron. He developed the so-called freeform method of expression in which he explored two main avenues — one was the usually solid 'immersion pieces' made up from many layers of glass, and the other was large, fat offhand forms developed by opening up asymmetrical bubbles and then generally stretched using the pincers.

Littleton's own work, having initially been quite free in form, soon developed in a very different way from the somewhat haphazard effects created by Labino. Littleton had already turned his back upon the much of what he had learned at Brighton under Braden. The concept of happy accident or what Leach himself called the fortuitous blemish, is found in his later work in glass. He uses glass as a sculptural medium and his works have little reference to vessel-forming methods or qualities. In glass he eventually freed himself from the designer/craftsman straightjacket.

Marvin Lipofsky followed in the footsteps of Peter Voulkos who was head of ceramics at Berkley. Like Voulkos he became interested in very asymmetrical lumpy forms before producing popular statements of often comic, even somewhat kitsch appearance in the 70s.

Sam Herman studied with Littleton and Labino in 1966. He came to England in 1969 and started teaching at the Royal College of Art where a furnace had been built back in 1963. Herman's work is very close to that of Labino and Littleton. In a seminar held at Brighton in 1984, Sam

Blown sculptural form, 'Butterfly Wing', by Harvey Littleton, 1969.

tute in the States and the UK.

At the 1984 Brighton Conference of the Decorative Arts Society, Sam Herman reiterated the principles of the new movement voiced earlier by Erwin Eisch in a lecture given to the Deutsche Glastechnische Gesellschaft in October 1975:

"We must recognize the essential rules of the material, respect them and work within them. We are interested only in the result of our work. The fluid material must receive breath, meaning and form – a form that for us clarifies and reflects the spirit of our time."

It is almost an echo of John Ruskin, writing over 100 years earlier in 1853 in *The Stones of Venice*, where he said:

Blown sculptural form with hot-metal additions by Sam Herman, 1965.

Herman emphasized the need to respond freely to the material. He opened the Glasshouse in the 1970s near Covent Garden in an area that was fast becoming an important centre of the designed arts in London.

Herman went to Australia in 1976 and founded the New Wave movement there. Since the early 70s the influence of the movement has spread as a result of similar missionary-like ventures. Of special importance in spreading the message have been the exhibitions of New Glass mounted by the Corning Insti-

"..all very neat, finished and perfect form in glass is barbarous: for this fails in proclaiming another of its great virtues; namely the ease with which its light substance can be moulded or blown into any form so

long as perfect accuracy be not required...but only such fantastic fickle grace as the mind of the work-man can conceive and execute on the instant...No material is so adapted to giving full play to the imagination.."

Left: Blown forms with marvered hot-metal decoration by Dominick Labino, 1960s.

BIBLIOGRAPHY

ARTS COUNCIL OF GREAT BRITAIN *The Thirties: British Art and Great Britain. Design Before the War* Exhibition catalogue, A.C.G.B, 1980.

ARWAS, V. *Glass – Art Nouveau to Art Deco* Rizzoli International, 1977.

BEARD, G. *Modern Glass* Studio Vista, 1958.

BEARD, G. *International Modern Glass* Barrie & Jenkins, 1976.

BLOCH-DERMANT, J. *The Art of French Glass: 1860-1914* Thames & Hudson, 1980.

CHARLESTON, R.J. *English Glass and the Glass used in England: c.400-1940.* Allen & Unwin, 1984.

CORNING MUSEUM OF GLASS *Glass 59: A Special Exhibition of International Contempory Glass* The Corning Museum of Glass, 1980.

DAUM, N. *Daum – Maitres Verriers* Edita Denoel, 1980.

DRAHOTOVA, O. *European Glass* Peerage Books, 1983.

DUNCAN, G.S. *A Bibliography of Glass* Society of Glass Technology, 1961

ELVILLE E.M. *The Collector's Dictionary of Glass* Country Life, 1961.

GARDNER, P. *The Glass of Frederick Carder* Crown, 1971.

GARNER, P. *Emile Gallé* Academy, 1976.

GROVER, R. & L. *European Art Glass Nouveau* Crown, 1967.

GROVER, R. & L. *Contemporary Art Glass* Crown, 1975.

JANNEAU, G. *Modern Glass* Studio, 1931

KLEIN, D. & WARD, L. *The History of Glass* Orbis, 1984.

KOCH, R. *Louis C. Tiffany: Rebel in Glass* Crown, 1964.

LABINO, D. *Decade of Glass Craftsmanship 1964–1974* Victoria & Albert Museum, 1974.

LALIQUE *Catalogue des Verreries de René Lalique.* René Lalique & Co., 1932.

LITTLETON, H.K. *Glassblowing: A Search for Form* Van Nostrand, 1972.

McFADDEN, D. *Scandinavian Modern Design* Harry. N. Abrams, 1982.

MORRIS, B. *Victorian Table Glass and Ornaments* Barrie & Jenkins, 1978.

MURRAY, K. *'The Design of Table Glass'* Design for Today, June 1933.

PAZAUREK, G.E. & SPIEGL, W. *Glas des 20 Jahrhunderts. Jungendstil – Art Deco* Klinkhardt & Biermann, 1983.

PEVSNER, N. *An Enquiry into Industrial Art in England* C.U.P., 1937.

POLAK, A. *Modern Glass* Faber, 1962.

POLAK, A. *Glass: Its Tradition and its Makers* Putnam's Sons, 1975.

RABIN, J. & MATURA, A. *Modern Bohemian Glass* Artia, 1980.
REVI, A.C. *Nineteenth Century Glass: Its Genesis and Its Development* Nelson, 1967.
REVI, A.C. *American Art Nouveau Glass* Nelson, 1968.
SCHWEIGER, WERNER J. *Wiener Werkstätte Kunst und Handwerk, 1903–1932* Thames & Hudson, 1984.
SPILLMAN, J.S. *The Cut and Engraved Glass of Corning, 1868–1940* Corning Museum of Glass, 1977.
SPILLMAN, J.S. *American and European Pressed Glass in the Corning Museum of Glass* Corning Museum of Glass, 1981.
STEENBERG, E. *Modern Swedish Glass* Lindqvist, 1949.
STEUBEN GLASS *British Artists in Crystal* Steuben Glass Co., 1954.
STEUBEN GLASS *The Story of Steuben Glass* Steuben Glass Co.
TOLEDO MUSEUM OF GLASS *Art in Glass* Toledo Museum, USA 1969.
ARTIGIANA VENEZIA *Vetri Murano Oggi* Exhibition catalogue, Murano Museum of Glass, 1981
VENETIAN CHAMBER OF COMMERCE *Glass in Murano* Exhibition catalogue, Venetian Chamber of Commerce & Artigiana Venezia, 1984.
VOSE, R.H. *Glass* Collins, 1980.
WEISS, G. *The Book of Glass* Barrie & Jenkins, 1971.

PERIODICALS:

AMERICAN

China, Glass and Tableware
Crockery and Glass Trades Journal
Journal of Glass Studies
Pottery and Glassware Reporter

ENGLISH

The Art Journal
Design Magazine
Glass Technology
Journal of the Society of Glass Technology
Pottery and Glass
Pottery Gazette and Glass Trades Review
The Studio
Tableware International

ACKNOWLEDGEMENTS

T = top; B = bottom; R = right; L = left

The author would like to thank Nicholas Sullivan for his invaluable support.

The author and publishers would also like to thank the following for their permission to reproduce the photographs on the pages listed: The Trustees of the British Museum: page 34TR; Broadfield House: pages 24, 34L, 66, 70, 99T; Cooper-Hewitt Museum: page 25; The Corning Museum of Glass, Corning, New York: pages title, 38BL, 41, 47L, 53; Dartington Glass Ltd: pages 80, 81, 82; Design Council: pages 72B, 73, 76–7, 78, 79TL; Holmegaard Glassworks: page 87; International Modern Glass and Modern Glass by Geoffrey Beard (Barrie & Jenkins): pages 28, 50R, 97; Karhula Iittala Glassworks: page 52R, 84, 85; Libbey Glass: pages 101B, 102T; Department of Art History, University of Manchester: pages 30–1; Meyrs Neffe: page 39L; Museum of Decorative Arts, Prague: pages cover, 37R, 44, 90, 107; National Scottish Museum: page 23; AB Orrefors Glasbruk: page 51T; Oslo Museum of Applied Art: page 51B; Pietro Raffo: page 26, 29B, 86T; Ravenhead Glass: page 75, 79TR; Rosenthal China Ltd: page 93, 94–5, 98, 99B; Royal Copenhagen: pages 88, 89; Steuben Glass: pages 54T, B, 56, 57, 58, 103; Sunderland Museum and Art Gallery: pages 62–3; Thomas Webb Crystal: pages 4, 79BL; Toledo Museum of Art: pages 101B, 102T; The Trustees of the Victoria and Albert Museum: pages 29T, 35TR, 47T,B, 64, 65, 69, 100, 102B; The Trustees of the Wedgwood Museum, Barlaston, Staffordshire: page 34BR and the Tyne and Wear Museum: pages 60, 61R, 72T and 74–5.

INDEX